Archaeology without Digging

Connecticut history uncovered by ground-penetrating radar

Deborah Surabian, Nick Bellantoni
and James Doolittle

OXBOW | books
Oxford & Philadelphia

Published in the United Kingdom in 2023 by
OXBOW BOOKS
The Old Music Hall, 106-108 Cowley Road, Oxford, OX4 1JE

and in the United States by
OXBOW BOOKS
1950 Lawrence Road, Havertown, PA 19083

Paperback Edition: ISBN 978-1-78925-926-1
Digital Edition: ISBN 978-1-78925-927-8

A CIP record for this book is available from the British Library

Library of Congress Control Number: 2023932440

Printed in the United Kingdom by CMP Digital Print Solutions

For a complete list of Oxbow titles, please contact:

UNITED KINGDOM
Oxbow Books
Telephone (0)1226 734350
Email: oxbow@oxbowbooks.com
www.oxbowbooks.com

UNITED STATES OF AMERICA
Oxbow Books
Telephone (610) 853-9131, Fax (610) 853-9146
Email: queries@casemateacademic.com
www.casemateacademic.com/oxbow

Oxbow Books is part of the Casemate Group

Front cover: All three authors working together on a cemetery project, John J. Spaulding.
Back cover: A Web Soil Survey map showing the area surrounding the Old Judea Cemetery.

Contents

List of illustrations

Acknowledgements

The authors wish to our gratitude to the following individuals and organizations for their participation and volunteerism for the each of the following surveys:

Stonington
Bruce Greene, Friends of the Office of State Archaeology Inc.

Old Norwichtown Burying Grounds
Jon Fuller, Graham Fuller, Bill Champagne, Patrice Champagne, Regan Miner, Norwichtown District Commission, Deanna Rhodes, Dale Plummer, Ruthie Brown, Scott Brady, Brian Jones

Judea Cemetery – Washington, CT
Mike Bird, Connecticut Society of the Sons of the American Revolution, Craig Nelson, the town of Washington, the Institute for American Indian Studies, Peter Stothart, Duncan Woodruff, Scott Brady

North Burying Ground, Danbury, CT
Scott Brady, Robert 'Bob' Young, Ronald Beckett, Ed Siergiej

Barkhamsted Lighthouse
Paul Hart, Barkhamsted Historical Society, Kristina Napolitano, Mike Day, Noreen Watson, Georgia Nash, Brian Jones, Ken Feder, Marc Banks

Essex, CT
Bruce Greene, Marissa Theve, Amy Trout, Connecticut River Museum

Middletown, CT
Scott Brady, August 'Augie' DeFrance

Bradley
Shawn McVey, Tom Palshaw, New England Air Museum, Paul Scannell, John Spalding, Roger Thompson, Captain Nick Hurley, Bradley International Airport, CT Department of Transportation

Windsor
Lori Kessel, George King IV, CT Archaeology Museum of Natural History, CT Archaeology Center's Field School, Monica Warson, Elizabeth Roberge, Greg Wanamaker, Emily Zepp, Sarah Breault, Mike Oldziej, Abbie Phillips, Brian Jones

We extend a special thanks to the Friends of the Office of State Archaeology Inc., whose volunteers assisted on every one of these GPR projects and the Connecticut River Museum, New England Air Museum, Bob Young and John J. Spaulding for use of their photographic collections and Bill Keegan for the map. Finally, we are grateful for the support of our editors at Oxbow Books, Julie Gardiner and Jessica Hawxwell, and graphic designer, Declan Ingram, who have demonstrated patience and sound judgement in seeing this book to conclusion.

Preface

The concept for this compilation of geophysical case studies applying ground-penetrating radar (GPR) technology as a research tool toward an understanding of archaeological and historical sites stems from over 20 years of field surveys the authors have conducted in Connecticut. Since soil conditions are favorable for GPR surveys in our state, the technology has been variously used to assess wetland conditions, reconstruct past coastlines, understand bedrock geology, and as a non-destructive technique for archaeological surveys.

Among the general public and students, particular interest has been elicited from our archaeological and historical studies. As a part of our surveys across the state, people have been fascinated by how the equipment works and how we are able to interpret historical events and discover unseen graves and buried features without having to excavate – archaeology without digging. Compelling historical narratives, including the discovery of unmarked pandemic burials, lost tombs, plane crashes, and other historical mysteries, have added human stories to these geophysical undertakings and highlight the importance of GPR in archaeological research.

The book is organized to provide a working introduction to GPR and archaeology with relevant case studies gleaned from our research projects. Our hopes are that this book will assist the general public in understanding how GPR operates and is applied in the field; educate the student with relevant case studies incorporating geophysical technique; and assist the professional in assessing interpretation of data recovered from GPR. Hence, we have written the text for an audience with wide interests in the field and hope *Archaeology without Digging* contributes to the body of work in this fascinating and ever-developing technological discipline.

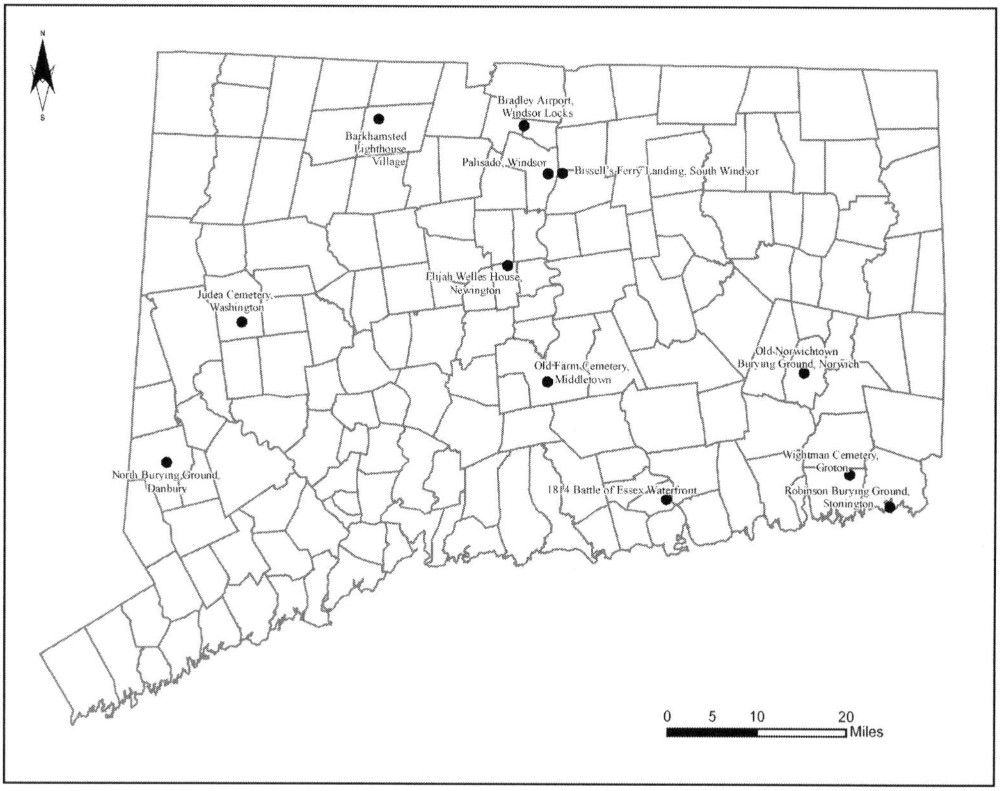

Map of the state of Connecticut showing the approximated locations of the sites discussed in this book (Map Credit: Bill Keegan).

Chapter 1

Use of ground-penetrating radar for cultural resource assessments

Ground-penetrating radar (GPR) is a geophysical method that uses electromagnetic energy to provide images of the subsurface. In Connecticut, we have used GPR for the assessment, preservation, and management of both known and unknown subsurface features at historical sites. In these endeavors, GPR has been used to detect, identify, and locate buried archaeological features; facilitate excavation strategies; provide greater areal coverage per unit time and cost; and minimize the number of unsuccessful exploratory excavations. As a non-destructive method, GPR has helped to preserve and avoid disturbing historical sites and buried features.

At many sites, the efficacy of archaeological investigations has been improved through the use of GPR with traditional field methods. The low clay and soluble salt contents of most Connecticut soils provide excellent conditions for deep and high-resolution profiling with GPR. However, not all investigations have been successful. At some historical sites, the condition and/or small size of the buried features, the high electrical conductivity of the soil, the presence of unwanted scattering bodies in the subsurface, and the lack of dielectric contrast between the buried artifacts and the host soil materials have posed significant challenges.

Principles of operation

Ground-penetrating radar is an impulse, or ultra-wideband, radar system that is designed to propagate electromagnetic energy into the underlying earthen materials and provide a visual representation of the subsurface. GPR transmits short pulses of high to ultra-high frequency (center frequencies from 12.5 MHz to 2.6 GHz) electromagnetic energy into the ground from an antenna that is moved along the ground surface. These pulses of electromagnetic energy form expanding wavefronts that move downward through the subsurface. As a wavefront spreads downwards through the subsurface, energy is dissipated (spreading loss and attenuation) until it is completely consumed. Rates of signal attenuation vary and depend on the physical and chemical properties of the subsurface materials through which the wavefronts spread (Leach 2021, 92). When a wavefront impinges upon a layer or object that has a contrasting relative dielectric permittivity (E_r; see below), a portion of the energy is reflected back to the receiving antenna. The more abrupt and contrasting the difference in E_r across a boundary or interface, the greater the amount of energy that is reflected back to the receiving antenna and the greater the amplitude of the reflection recorded in the radar data.

Dielectric permittivity is the ability of a material to store and release electromagnetic energy in the form of an electrical charge (Cassidy 2009). Relative dielectric permittivity, or dielectric constant, is the ratio of the permittivity of a substance to that of free space (vacuum with E_r of 1). Relative dielectric permittivity ranges from 1 for air to 78–88 for water (Cassidy 2009). As such, E_r is strongly dependent upon moisture content, but is also affected by temperature (phase-dependent), density, and antenna frequency (Daniels 2004, 726).

The energy that is reflected back to an antenna from the subsurface is assembled into digital scans or traces with the amplitude of the received signals represented by either a color scale or greyscale on a line scan image, or oscillations on either side of a zero-amplitude line on an O-scope style display. As an antenna is moved along the ground surface, a continuous stream of vertical scans is collected to form a radar profile or record. The collected radar data are shown on a display screen for in-the-field interpretations, and stored on a hard drive or flash memory card in the control console for future playback and/or processing.

GPR is a time-scaled system that measures the time taken for the pulses of electromagnetic energy to travel from an antenna to an interface and back. To convert this travel time into a depth scale, either the depth to an identifiable interface or the propagation velocity of the electromagnetic pulses through the subsurface must be known. This relationship is described by the equation:

$$D = VT/2 \qquad (1)$$

where D is the depth to an interface; V is the velocity of pulse propagation; and T is the two-way travel time of the electromagnetic pulse to the interface, which is measured in nanoseconds (ns). A nanosecond is a billionth of a second or 10^{-9} seconds. The depth to an interface that appears on a radar profile is most accurately determined by direct coring or excavating to the feature (if possible), whereby its actual depth can be measured. As the two-way travel time to a feature can be measured on the radar profile, the velocity of pulse propagation can then be determined using its known depth and equation (1). Once the velocity of pulse propagation is calculated, this value is used to determine the relative dielectric permittivity of the medium through which the pulse has traveled according to equation (2):

$$E_r = (C/V)^2 \qquad (2)$$

where C is the propagation velocity in free space (3×10^8 m/sec or 1 ft/ns). The calculated E_r is then entered into a menu on the radar's control console, whereby a depth scale for the entire radar profile is calculated and displayed. As E_r is spatially and temporally variable, and dependent on the composition and thickness of the profiled earthen materials, the depth scale shown on a radar profile is only an approximation.

In sensitive areas and wherever digging is not possible to measure the depth to an interface, a processing technique known as migration can be utilized to estimate the velocity of pulse propagation from the shape of hyperbolic reflections appearing on the radar profile. By employing the 'hyperbola matching' method, an average dielectric permittivity is determined and used to estimate a suitable depth scale for the radar profile.

Compared with other geophysical techniques, GPR provides the highest resolution of subsurface features. Resolution refers to both the size of smallest object that can be detected and the ability to differentiate between two closely-spaced features. Resolution is dependent on the antenna frequency, the velocity of pulse propagation, and the distance of a feature from an antenna. Resolution increases with antenna frequency. Higher frequency antennas have shorter wavelengths, which provide better resolution of smaller and/or more closely-spaced features. Resolution increases with decreasing velocity of pulse propagation. Lower propagation velocities result in shorter wavelengths with more focused energy and improved resolution of subsurface features. The velocity of pulse propagation is inversely related to the dielectric permittivity of the profiled materials; a higher E_r results in lower V and more focused radiation patterns. Resolution decreases with depth. The greater the distance or depth to a feature, the more distorted and wider the cross-sectional area of the propagated wavefront. Leach (2021) observed that 'for every 30 cm (1 ft) of depth an object's size must increase by 2.5 cm (1 inch)' to be detectable with either a 200 or 500 MHz center frequency antenna.

While higher frequency antennas provide greater resolution of subsurface features than lower frequency antennas, they are more depth restricted. Pulses of electromagnetic energy from higher frequency antennas are more rapidly attenuated by subsurface materials than those from lower frequency antennas. As a consequence, higher frequency antennas (>350 MHz) are more limited in their profiling depths than lower frequency antennas (<300 MHz).

The GPR system

The ground-penetrating radar data acquisition systems used by the authors are the SIR (Subsurface Interface Radar)-3000 and the SIR-4000, both manufactured by Geophysical Survey Systems, Inc (GSSI; Nashua, NH).[1] The more recently developed SIR-4000 data acquisition system (Fig. 1.1) can operate with both digital and analog antennas. The older SIR-3000 operates with analog antennas only. Both systems have control consoles that consist of a signal processor, data storage unit, display screen, keypad, and connector panel. These light weight (9–10 lb/c. 4–4.5 kg), highly portable units are powered by a 10.8-volt lithium-ion rechargeable battery. While GSSI manufactures antennas that are nominally rated to operate at center frequencies ranging from 16 to 2600 MHz, we have found the 400, 500, and 900 MHz analog antennas and the 350 MHz digital antenna to be the most appropriate for investigating historical sites in Connecticut. These antennas provide suitable investigation depths and resolution of buried historical features in most Connecticut soils. Typically, these antennas are either placed in a survey cart that is equipped with an encoder or have a survey wheel attached for accurate distance measurements. For investigations conducted without a survey cart or wheel, the GPR data acquisition system (i.e., control console) is attached to a carrying harness that is fitted to the operator. For investigations conducted in more inhospitable sites and terrains, where neither the survey cart or wheel can be used, GPR traverses are conducted along lines having measured distance marks or survey flags set at fixed distances.

The SIR-3000 and SIR-4000 data acquisition systems have Windows based user interfaces and include signal processing and display capabilities for 'in-the-field' viewing (Fig. 1.2). As shown in Figure 1.2, radar data are displayed in line scan and O-scope formats. These radar systems can be integrated with a global positioning system (GPS) to record the location of the antenna as it is moved along the ground surface.

Data processing

The windows based RADAN® post-processing software, developed by GSSI, has been used to improve radar interpretations.[2] This software is designed to process, view, and document data collected with the SIR systems. Basic processing procedures commonly used include Time-Zero Correction; Background Removal; and Color Table, Color Transform and Display Gain parameters selection. Time-Zero Correction is used to adjust vertically the position of the entire radar profile by moving the time-zero position (center of first positive peak) of the ground wave to the top of the profile. This correction provides more accurate depth calculations by adjusting the top of the radar scan to a close approximation of the ground surface. Background Removal is a filter that removes horizontal bands of noise from radar profiles. These horizontal bands are often caused by low frequency noise that can obscure other 'real' horizontal or point source reflectors. Color Table and Color Transform parameter selections are used to enhance the data displayed. Color tables are used to color-code the amplitudes on radar scans. The Color Transform is used to enhance weak amplitudes from less contrasting reflectors. Display Gain is used to enhance and make it easier to see lower amplitude reflections.

When data are collected with the SIR data acquisition system without a survey cart or wheel, Distance Normalization is used to adjust the horizontal time scale into a distance scale. This is required because of the unavoidable inconsistencies in the

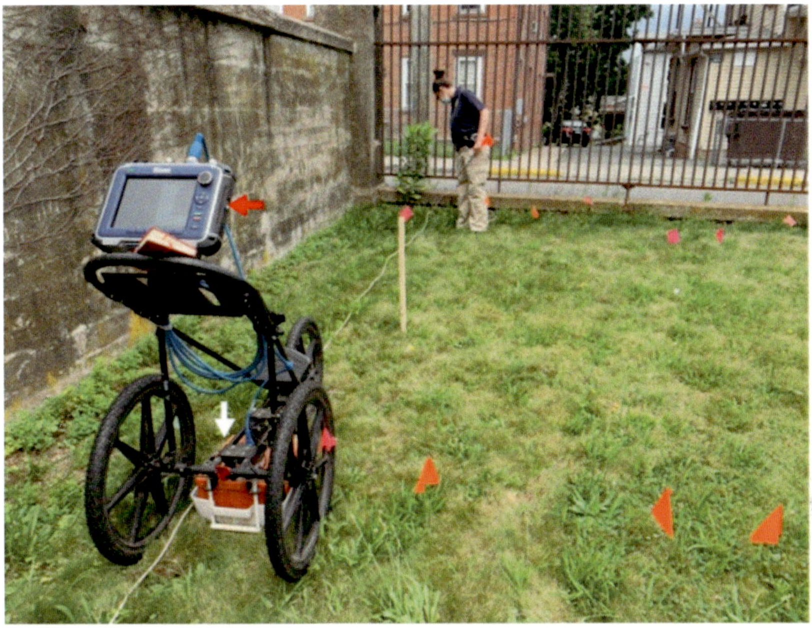

Fig. 1.1: An SIR-4000 (red arrow) attached to survey cart with a 400 MHz antenna (white arrow) is positioned to conduct a survey at the Mortimer Cemetery in Middletown, Connecticut.

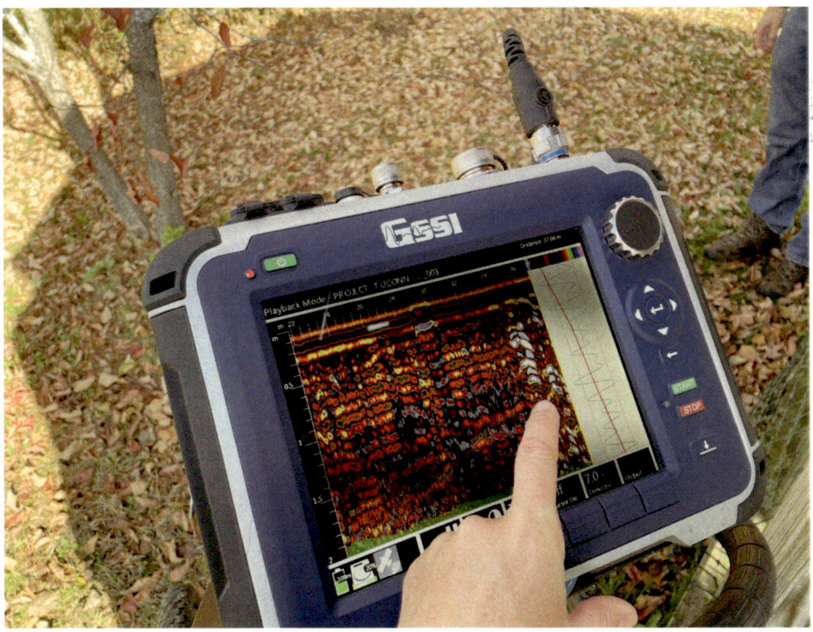

Fig. 1.2: A 2D radar profile (on left) and single scan O-scope style display of a single point along a traverse line (on extreme right) are displayed on an SIR 4000.

speed of antenna advance. When Distance Normalization is used, distance marker information must be inserted in the collected radar data. Distance Normalization will correct the number of scans between these markers by stretching and skipping, thereby correcting for variations in survey speed.

Radar profiles and depth-slice images

As an antenna is moved along the ground surface, a continuous stream of subsurface data is collected and displayed on the screen of the control console. In Figure 1.2, a recorded radar profile (in line scan format) of the subsurface along a traverse line (left), and a single-scan, O-scope style display of a position (right) along this line are shown on the video screen of the control console. In both presentations, time and depth increase down the screen.

A radar profile is a two-dimensional (2D) image of the subsurface along a GPR traverse line. A radar profile is similar to the exposed sidewall of an excavated trench with vertical exaggeration. On a typical radar profile, the horizontal scale is distance-based, and the vertical scale is expressed as either the two-way travel time or the estimated depth. The ground surface is at the top of the radar profile, with reflections from the subsurface below. On most radar profiles, the horizontal scale is compressed relative to the vertical scale. Using a line scan format, radar reflections are displayed as bands of differing colors based on the color table selected. Each radar reflection consists of alternating bands of positive and negative pulse polarity. The amplitude of the reflected signal is displayed in different assigned colors or color intensities (greyscale).

Figure 1.3 contains an unprocessed and a processed image of the same radar profile that was collected across a set of seven graves in the Milford Cemetery, Milford, Connecticut. The GPR data were collected with a 400 MHz antenna that was set to scan to an approximated depth of about 2.5 m. On the radar profiles shown in Figure 1.3, the vertical scales represent depth (time scale has been converted to a depth scale). The horizontal scales represent the distance traveled along the traverse line by the radar antenna. Both scales are expressed in meters (m). Both radar profiles display the reflected signals in a conventional line scan format. A greyscale color table has been used, which displays a continuous range of grey shades from white to black. The greyscale assigns white and black colors to the highest positive and negative electromagnetic pulse polarities, respectively. Variations in the intensity of reflection amplitudes are shown in shades of grey.

In Figure 1.3, the profile on the left is the raw, unprocessed data that was collected in the field. The profile on the right has been processed using two standard processing techniques: Time-Zero Correction and Background Removal. In Figure 1.3, the unprocessed radar profile has an added, dashed, black-colored horizontal line, which identifies the approximate time-zero position. The radar profile on the right has the time-zero position adjusted and shifted to the top of the profile. On this radar

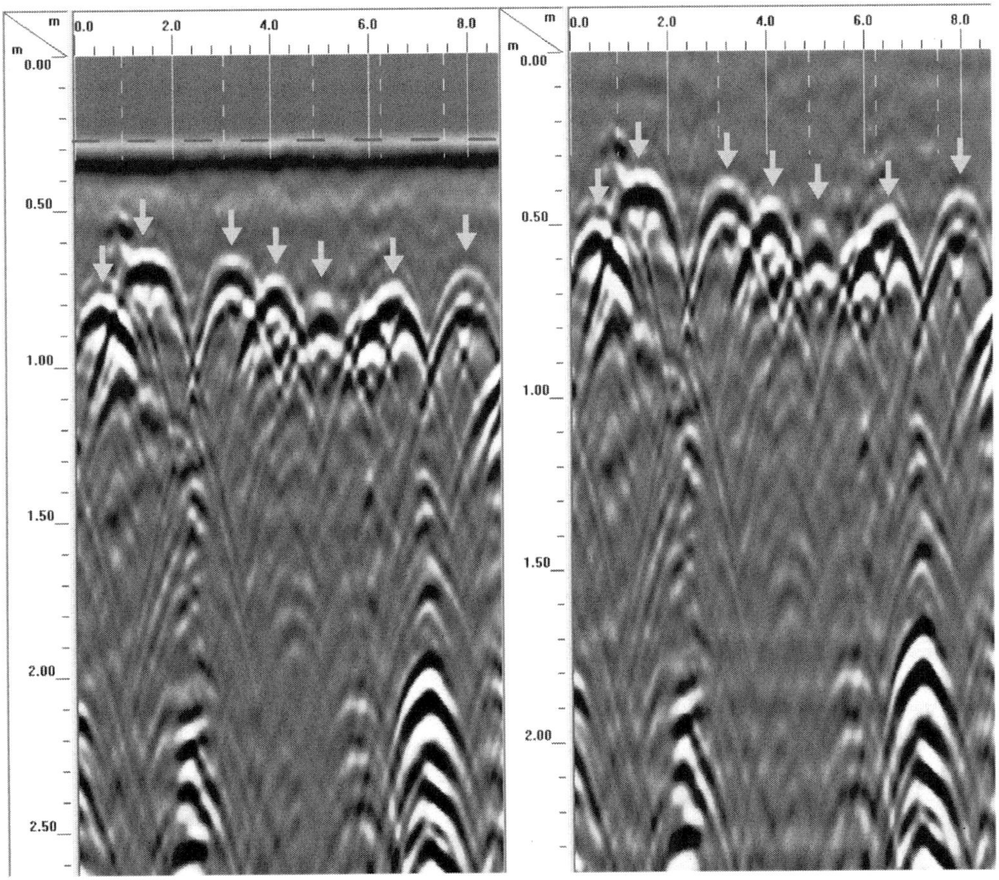

Fig. 1.3: 'Raw' (left) and processed (right) radar profiles of the same traverse across a family plot in the Milford Cemetery, Milford, Connecticut.

profile, a background removal filter has also been used to remove unwanted horizontal bands of low frequency noise; most noticeably the strong reflection caused by the air/ground surface interface.

On both radar profiles, seven point-source anomalies, each representing a subsurface feature, have been identified by the inserted, white arrows. Reflections from small, point source objects form hyperbolic patterns. Hyperbolic reflections are caused by the wide angle of the transmitted wavefront and the antenna sensing a point-source object at a greater distance both before and after it passes over it. The apex of a hyperbola represents the location of a point source object. Point-source objects include small rock fragments, bricks, voids, and artifacts. They also include buried walls, pipes, or coffins that are passed over by the antenna in a direction that is essentially perpendicular to their long axis. When GPR traverses are conducted over and parallel to the long axis of these extended features, they often appear as continuous, linear bands of reflections. However, these linear reflection patterns can also represent segments of natural structural boundaries such as soil horizons, stratigraphic layers, and lithological contacts.

The radar profile shown in Figure 1.3 captures an 8.5 m traverse that was conducted parallel with a line of seven headstones. The recorded years of death inscribed on the headstones are (from left to right): 1959, 1971, 1986, 1958, 2008, 1968, and 1962. In this example, the seven identified reflection anomalies represent these burials. The high amplitudes and shallow depths to these anomalies were attributed to their recent interments and the use of reinforced concrete burial vaults or liners.

Amplitude time-slice imagery

The effective processing and visualization of radar data is the key to GPR interpretations. Amplitude time-slice analysis, an advanced type of GPR data manipulation, is commonly used to image variations in reflection amplitude patterns at different scanning times or depths across a gridded area (Conyers and Goodman 1997, 232; Conyers 2013). For this analysis, a 3D data volume of the subsurface is created by the computer processing and synthesis of a series of closely spaced, 2D radar profiles that were collected across a gridded site. Amplitude differences in the constructed 3D data volume are then analyzed in horizontally sliced images of the subsurface that show changes in reflection amplitudes within specified time or depth intervals (Conyers and Goodman 1997). In this process, the reflected radar energy is averaged horizontally between the closely spaced, parallel radar profiles and in specified time (or depth) windows to create time-slice (or depth-slice) images. Each amplitude time-slice image shows the spatial distribution of reflected wave amplitudes across a gridded area, which can indicate changes in the properties of soils; the structures of soil, stratigraphic and lithologic features; and the presence of buried cultural features. In archaeological studies, depth-slice amplitude images have been used to show the locations, depths, distributions, and geometries of buried structures and features from different perspectives and cross-sections (Conyers 2011; 2013).

The construction of depth-slice images requires a relatively small area (usually, 1–2500 m^2) to be intensively surveyed with multiple, closely spaced, parallel GPR grid lines. The grid line interval is determined by the structure(s) or feature(s) being search for, the size of the survey area, and the resources available. In general, a relatively dense array of grid lines is necessary to resolve the geometries and sizes of different subsurface features and to prevent spatially aliasing the data (Grasmueck and Green 1996). As a general rule, the smaller the size of the targeted feature, the closer the required grid line spacing. Once collected, the composite radar data are processed into a 3D data volume (Fig. 1.4, left) of the grid site, from which arbitrary cross-sections, insets, and time-slices (Fig. 1.4, right) can be extracted. Interactive software packages enable these images to be viewed from nearly any perspective on a computer (Junck and Jol 2000).

Figure 1.4 contains a 3D data volume display (left) and three depth-slice amplitude images (right) from the aforementioned family plot in the Milford Cemetery (Milford, Connecticut). The 3D data volume defines a rectangular grid area with horizontal dimensions of 8.5 × 2.0 m. The profiling depth is about 2.5 m. The 3D volume was developed from GPR data collected along nine, equally spaced (25 cm), parallel grid lines that spanned the site. A radar profile from one of these nine grid lines is shown in Figure 1.3. The three depth-slice amplitude images were extracted from depths of about 0 cm, 70 cm, and 210 cm. In our Connecticut studies, we have typically used slices that range in thickness from about 18 cm to 25 cm, with one-half of the slice thickness above and below the indicated slice depth.

In Figure 1.4, the shallowest (0 cm) depth-slice amplitude image is nondescript, being uniformly black with an absences of reflection patterns. These conditions indicate relatively uniform and homogenous soil materials with a lack of contrasting features. On the 70 cm depth-slice image, the narrow, elongated, high-amplitude (colored mostly white, dark red and blue) reflection patterns are believed to represent the sidewalls of seven, shallowly buried, concrete burial vaults or liners. On the 210 cm depth-slice amplitude image, the two elongated, high amplitude reflection patterns are believed to represent the ringing or reverberations of reflected signals off the sidewalls of overlying, closely spaced burial vaults or liners. The remaining area of this depth-slice image consists of several dispersed and irregularly shaped reflection patterns that are assumed to represent inhomogeneities within the underlying glacial outwash.

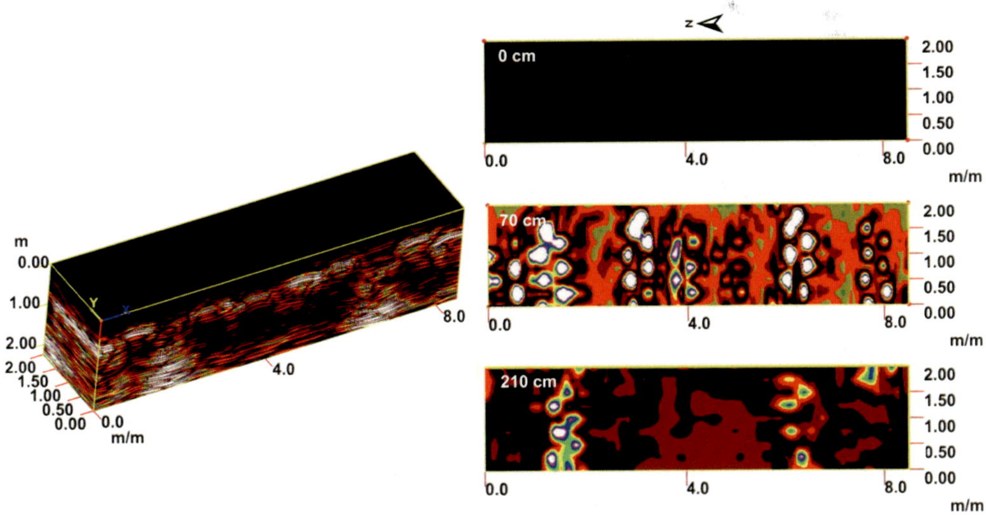

Fig. 1.4: A 3D radar data volume (left) and three depth-slice amplitude images (right) of a family plot in the Milford Cemetery, Milford, Connecticut.

Survey procedures

The most accepted and, perhaps, most efficient method of detecting and charting the location of buried historical features with GPR is to establish a grid composed of closely spaced, parallel lines across a site. The grid interval is a compromise among the purpose of the survey, size of the area to be surveyed, features being identified, available resources, desired detection probability, and required positional accuracy. In the survey of historical sites in Connecticut, we have used rectangular grids with a grid or traverse line spacing ranging from 0.25 m to 1.0 m.

To facilitate the construction of grids, two parallel survey lines are laid out on opposing sides of the proposed grid area, defining its boundaries. Along each of these two opposing grid boundary lines, survey flags are inserted into the ground or chalk marks are drawn (on paved areas) at a uniform interval (either 25 cm, 50 cm, or 100 cm). Beginning at the designated grid origin, a rope or tapeline is stretched between corresponding survey flags or chalk marks that are located on the opposing boundary lines. The GPR antenna is moved along this line for guidance while collecting subsurface data (Fig. 1.5). Following data collection along this grid line, the rope or tapeline is sequentially moved to the next pair of corresponding survey flags or chalk marks on the opposing boundary lines to repeat the process. The radar traverses are completed by using either a back-and-forth or a single direction of advance across the grid. Data collected along each GPR traverse line is saved as a separate file on the hard drive or a flash memory card in the control console for record, display, and processing purposes.

Grids are established over areas that are relatively free of obstacles. If obstacles (e.g., trees, building, walls, boulders) are present, several smaller grids can be established to avoid these obstructions. Detailed handwritten notes, a rough map of the grid site with its geometry shown, as well as the location, direction of advance, and file numbers of the GPR traverses are recorded in a notebook.

Line or random walk GPR surveys (Fig. 1.6) have been conducted to reconnoiter quickly large, relatively unknown, and/or more inhospitable terrains for historical features. These surveys are often conducted to locate anomalous and noteworthy reflection patterns. Line or random walk surveys are exploratory in nature and focus on identifying potential areas of interest where more intensive surveys and/or field examinations can be conducted. However, they result in a higher degree of uncertainty than the more area-restrictive, time-consuming, methodical, and comprehensive grid surveys. Unfortunately, we have often found that random walk surveys result in far more misses than successes.

Suitability of Connecticut soils for ground-penetrating radar

The effectiveness of GPR is highly site-specific and soil dependent. Results vary with soils properties and site conditions. Soils having high electrical conductivity rapidly attenuate radar energy, restrict penetration depths, and limit the effectiveness of GPR.

The electrical conductivity of soils will increase with increases in water, clay, and/or soluble salt contents. As a consequence, most relatively dry, sandy (<15% clay) soils that have low soluble salt contents are considered well suited to high resolution and deep profiling with GPR. Conversely, most relatively wet, clayey (≥35% clay) soils and soils with high soluble salt contents (saturated extract electrical conductivity ≥4 dS m^{-1} at 25°C) are considered poorly suited to GPR because of their high electrical conductivity and rates of signal attenuation (Doolittle *et al.* 2007).

Soils are spatially variable. Significant changes in soil properties, hydrology, and parent materials can occur over short distances and impact the effective use of GPR. One hundred and seventeen different soils are presently identified in Connecticut (CT DEEP and USDA NRCS 2022). These soils occur in 369 different soil map units that are recognized across the state (Soil Survey Staff 2022). Each soil map unit is composed of one or more named soils that occur together in a particular landscape. Soil map units are named according to their principal soil components or miscellaneous areas. Miscellaneous areas (e.g., Beaches, Dumps, Pits, Quarries, Rock outcrop, Urban land, and Water) have essentially no recognized soil and are the result of active erosion, washing by water, unfavorable soil conditions, as well as removal, filling or covering by human activities, structures and/or roads.

Prior to conducting a GPR investigation, the Web Soil Survey[3] and soil series descriptions[4] can be used to better understand the relative suitability of the soils within the site for GPR, select the most suitable antennas, and assess the need and level of data processing. In addition, interpretations are frequently improved with knowledge of the underlying soil and geologic structures and features that should be apparent on radar profiles and depth-slice images.

The Ground-Penetrating Radar Soil Suitability Map of Connecticut (Fig. 1.7) shows the relative suitability of soils within the state for the use of GPR. This map was prepared by the United States Department of Agriculture – Natural Resources Conservation Service (USDA-NRCS) and is based on soil attribute data contained in the Soil Survey Geographic (SSURGO) database. The relative suitability ratings shown on this map are based principally on the clay and soluble salt contents of the dominant soils within each soil map unit. These ratings are limited as they do not account for spatial and temporal differences in soil moisture. Spatially, differences in relief and slope position result in differences in hydrology and soil moisture contents within map units. Temporally, soil moisture contents vary with weather patterns and seasons. As evident on this map, the vast majority of soils in Connecticut are rated as highly favorable for deep signal penetration and high resolution of subsurface features using a wide array of GPR antennas. The low clay and soluble salt contents of most Connecticut soils provide highly suitable mediums for the use of GPR at historical sites.

Connecticut is blanketed by a cover of glacial drift that consists of till, glaciofluvial, and glaciolacustrine deposits. Till consists of poorly sorted, unstratified drift that was deposited on, within, or beneath glacial ice. Soils formed in the tills of Connecticut

Fig. 1.5: Conducting a GPR grid survey on the Mohegan Reservation at Fort Shantok, Uncasville, Connecticut. Note the grid boundary line with survey flags spaced at 50 cm intervals (background) and the guideline (foreground) that is stretched between similarly numbered flags on the opposing grid boundary lines.

Fig. 1.6: Conducting a line or random walk survey across a relatively inaccessible and hostile terrain in search of a suspected a Colonial Army encampment site in Redding, Connecticut.

Fig. 1.7: A ground-penetrating radar soil suitability map of Connecticut.

have a mixed mineralogy, low clay contents (0–18%) and soil reactions that range from 3.5 to 6.5 (extremely acid to slightly acid). Soils formed in till include the loamy, very deep (>150 cm to bedrock), well drained Charlton, Cheshire, Montauk, Paxton, and Wethersfield series, and the shallow (<50 cm) and moderately deep (50–100 cm) to bedrock Hollis and Chatfield series, respectively. These soils have a very high potential for the use of GPR. The Montauk, Paxton, and Wethersfield soils form in relatively dense lodgment tills and are moderately deep to a densic contact (Cd horizon), which, though variable in expression, is discernable on most radar profiles. Densic contacts restrict the infiltration of water, which can accumulate along this contact for brief periods in late fall through early spring.

Glaciofluvial deposits consists of sorted, stratified drift that was deposited by meltwater streams flowing from glaciers. Soils formed in glaciofluvial sediments in Connecticut have a mixed mineralogy, low clay contents (0–18%) and soil reactions that range from 3.5 to 6.5 (extremely acid to slightly acid). Soils formed in glaciofluvial sediments include the very deep, well drained, loamy over sandy Agawam, Branford, and Haven series; the very deep, excessively or somewhat excessively drained, sandy or sandy-skeletal Hinckley, Manchester, Merrimac, and Windsor series. These soils are considered well suited to GPR.

In portions of the Connecticut River valley north of Rocky Hill, some very deep, moderately well drained to poorly drained soils (e.g., Berlin, Brancroft, Scitico, and Shaker series) occur. These soils formed in silty and clayey glaciolacustrine sediments that were deposited on the bottom of glacial Lake Hitchcock. The Berlin and Brancroft soils have clay contents that can range from 18% to 35%, and soil reactions that range from 5.1 to 7.3 (strongly acid to neutral). These soils are generally considered suited to most investigations with GPR. The poorly drained Scitico and Shaker soils have clay contents that are greater than 35% and soil reactions that range from 3.5 to 7.8 (extremely acid to slightly alkaline). Scitico and Shaker soils are typically saturated and have a water table that is at or near the surface throughout much of the year. These soils are considered to have a low potential for the use of GPR.

In coastal areas of Connecticut, some soils are affected by tidal actions and have high concentrations of soluble salts within depths of 50 cm (20 in). These soils have relatively high electrical conductivities and are generally considered unsuitable for GPR investigations. Major soils in tidal marshes, which are subjected to inundation by salt water, include the very deep, very poorly drained Ipswich, Pawcatuck, and Westbrook series. These organic soils are typically saturated with water, have soil reactions that range from 5.1 to 7.8 (strongly acid to slightly alkaline), and are slightly to strongly saline. The very deep, excessively drained, sandy Hooksan series formed in aeolian sands derived from sandy marine deposits on dunes along coastal beaches. Hooksan soils are considered very suitable for the use of GPR.

On the Connecticut GPR Soil Suitability Map, areas that are labeled 'No Data' lack soil property data in more than 50% of their area. These are miscellaneous areas that include quarries, rock outcrops, and some areas that covered by artificially modified materials (e.g., Borrow pits, Dumps, Made land, Paved areas, Urban land).

Soil properties control not only the profiling depths but also the effectiveness of GPR for the investigation of historical sites. Soil properties and features influence, and can constrain, radar interpretations. An understanding of the properties and structural architecture of soils at survey sites can aid GPR interpretations.

Connecticut soils are relatively youthful and generally lack well expressed soil horizons. Individual soil horizons (O, A, Ap, Bg, Bw, Bs, and BC horizons) are generally poorly expressed, lack sufficient contrast, and/or are generally too thin to be distinguished with GPR. Most Connecticut soils contain scattering bodies (e.g., soil inhomogeneities and disturbances, rock fragments, tree roots, animal burrows, modern cultural debris). Scattering bodies produce unwanted reflections that can clutter radar profiles and confound interpretations by concealing or obscuring the 'desired' reflections from buried historical features.

In many Connecticut soils, the glacial drift or bedrock is directly overlain by a comparatively homogenous, fine sand to silty sand, eolian mantle that is variable in thickness, but generally less than 1 m (3 ft) thick (Skehan 2008, 288). Where present, this eolian mantle is relatively homogenous and generally lacks the large number of rock fragments that are often prevalent in the glacial drift. As a consequence, the solum (upper part: O, A, E and B horizons) of mineral soils that develops in the eolian mantle will appear relatively homogenous and display a general absence of moderate and high amplitude reflections on radar profiles and depth-slice amplitude imagery. The contact separating the eolian mantle from the underlying glacial drift or bedrock is generally discernable on radar profiles.

Mineral soils that formed entirely in glacial drift will generally lack a prominent and well-defined interface separating the soil solum from the underlying substratum (C horizons) on radar profiles. However, on most radar profiles, a general distinction can be made between the soil solum and the relatively unaltered substratum based on differences in the number of scattering bodies and general appearance. In areas where the soil solum is underlain by dense till (Cd horizon) or bedrock (R), a high-amplitude, layered reflection pattern is often observed. This interface can have a smooth to undulating, or a highly irregular, broken appearance on radar profiles.

Soils formed in till are poorly sorted (i.e., having coarse fragments of many sizes that are mixed together in a chaotic manner) and contain unwanted reflections from scattering bodies. On radar profiles, these deposits have a jumbled appearance with numerous hyperbolic and some layered reflections. The hyperbolic reflections are largely produced by rock fragments of varying sizes, shapes, and lithologies. Layered reflection patterns generally represent the limited stratifications within these tills. These scattering bodies and layered reflections, while helpful in identifying the till, are often undesired as they complicate radar profiles and can mask the presence and challenge the recognition of buried historical features. It is a common experience for sought-after historical features to be partially concealed or even indistinguishable because of the background clutter that is inherent in tills.

Soils formed in glaciofluvial deposits have stratified layers of sands and gravels which produce layered reflection patterns on radar profiles. Larger stones and boulders can be present in glaciofluvial deposits. On radar profiles, the layered reflection patterns from these deposits display a wide range of reflection amplitudes with topographies that can range from plane and slightly inclined to highly irregular and broken. The abrupt truncation of these linear reflection patterns can provide indications of soil disturbance, excavations, and the location of possible historical features. However, some historical features can be masked on radar profiles collected in outwash deposits composed of multiple truncated strata of varying compositions, spatial extent, and inclinations. In these deposits, human structures may be difficult to distinguish from segmented, stratified layers of sands and gravel.

In many of Connecticut's urban settings, accessible areas for GPR surveys may be small, densely cluttered with rubble and debris, and/or consist of severely disturbed soils. Radar profiles collected in these settings may be overwhelmed by complex reflection patterns caused by a heterogenous mixture of soils, fill materials, and debris. This unwanted clutter can make the reliable identification of natural, historical, and modern subsurface features on radar profiles and images difficult if not impossible.

Contrasting reflection patterns are produced by areas of soil disturbances. Mixed soil materials are placed in refilled grave shafts, abandoned cellars, and derelict ditches. These mixed soil materials can provide contrasting reflection patterns which truncate layered soil horizons or geologic strata on some radar profiles and depth-slice amplitude images. These features contain mixed soil materials that are initially less dense and have dielectric properties that often contrast with the surrounding, undisturbed soil (Bevan 1991; Miller 1996; Doolittle and Bellantoni 2010). The detection of refilled grave shafts and excavations with GPR is more likely in soils with well-expressed soil horizons and/or geological strata. However, many Connecticut soils lack well-expressed soil horizons. As described above, soils formed in till consists of unsorted, unstratified, heterogenous sediments that produce cluttered and disorganized reflection patterns that can be similar to those in refilled graves and excavations. The abrupt vertical boundaries of these features have been most apparent where they cut across and disrupt the layered reflection patterns provided by stratified layers of glacial drift.

Soils are considered the repositories and control the preservation of historical features (Cummins *et al.* 2018). Soil properties influence rates of disintegration and what is preserved. Durable features such as buried stone foundation walls and concrete vaults are preserved for long periods of time and typically produce conspicuous reflections on radar profiles and depth-slice imagery. However, soil displacement caused by mass wasting, freeze-thaw processes, tree throw and root growth, and human activities can disrupt these features, causing their reflection patterns to be obscured on radar profiles and images.

The decomposition of bones and perishable features made of wood, cloth, or leather is influenced by microbial activity, soil reaction (pH), temperature, and moisture

(Surabian 2012). Bones and perishable features are rarely preserved in the acidic, free-draining soils of Connecticut where burials from the early 1900s have been observed to be completely decomposed in soils with pH of 4.7–4.9 while, in soils with pH above 5.5, burials from the 1700s were in a better state of preservation (Doolittle and Bellantoni 2010). It has been observed that older wooden coffins and bones buried in acidic, well drained soils leave little to no evidence other than grave goods, corroded shroud pins, coffin nails and hardware, and stains in soils (Surabian 2012). These remnant features are generally too small or lack sufficient contrast to be detected with GPR.

Kibblewhite and others (2015) and Cummins and others (2018) noted that bones decay rapidly in acidic, freely draining, aerobic soil environments, especially those formed in sands. These researchers also observed that the least preserving hydrological conditions for bones, perishable features, and metals are soils that have oxygenated water flowing through the soil profile. Seven natural soil drainage classes (i.e., excessively, somewhat excessively, well, moderately well, somewhat poorly, poorly, and very poorly drained) are recognized based on observations of the ability to allow the passage of both water and air, depth to water table, landscape position, and soil morphology (Connecticut Environmental Conditions Online 2010). The majority of the soils at historical sites described in the following chapters range from well drained to excessively drained and are very deep (>150 cm) to a water table and saturated soil conditions.

In summary, the majority of the soils found in Connecticut are considered well suited to deep profiling with a wide range of GPR antennas. While highly compatible to GPR, these soils contain scattering bodies and structures that produce unwanted reflections that can obscure reflections from buried historical features. These soils are mostly highly acidic and free draining; properties that compromise the preservation of bones and other perishable, buried features.

The soils found at each of the historical sites described in the following chapters will be discussed. These discussions will summarize pertinent soil properties that are considered important to GPR interpretations. This knowledge has proven helpful in the analysis of a site's suitability for the effectiveness use of GPR, the acknowledgement of possible uncertainties in the interpretation of results, and the assessment of the likelihood of success.

Notes

1 Manufacturer's names are provided for specific information; use does not constitute endorsement.
2 Manufacturer's names are provided for specific information; use does not constitute endorsement.
3 https://websoilsurvey.sc.egov.usda.gov/App/HomePage.htm
4 https://soilseries.sc.egov.usda.gov/osdname.aspx

Part I

Historical cemeteries

Chapter 2

The bomb crater burial of Hulda Hall, Robinson Burial Ground, Stonington

The shells were thrown, the rockets flew,
But not a shell of all they threw,
Though every house was in full view,
Could burn a house in Stonington

Philip Freneau: *The Battle of Stonington, On The Seaboard of Connecticut* (1814), recited in Palmer (1913, 41–4)

Regardless of Philip Freneau's optimistic poem commemorating the Battle of Stonington, many of the Borough's 120 houses, which were crowded on the narrow peninsula jutting into Long Island Sound, were heavily rattled by British cannons during the three-day barrage. Though none of these structures were totally destroyed or burned to the ground, the bombardment was, nevertheless, horrific.

The War of 1812, often referred to as the 'Second War for American Independence', was extremely unpopular in New England. It was derogatively labeled the 'Virginian's War' by many Connecticans, who saw the conflict as disapproval of President James Madison's (the Virginian) policies and the disruption to their once flourishing business trade with England and France, as well as a disaster for the country (Ellis 2009, 6). Since the end of the American Revolution, the state's maritime and mercantile industries were dependent on this trade. The return of war against Britain with its resultant embargos and interrupted trade meant possible bankruptcy for many of the state's businesses. So upset were many Federalist Party delegates to the Hartford Convention, which was convened in secrecy from 15 December 1814 to 5 January 1815 to express their grievances against President James Madison's administration, that some members strongly advocated secession from the Union should the War persist. Fortunately, more reasonable heads prevailed and the Convention would vote to stay and finish the War against England (Banner 1970).

At the time, Britain was immersed in the Napoleonic wars with France, giving rise to both nations blockading American shipments to their respective enemy. Compounding the situation, England had impressed over 10,000 American sailors unto British ships to supplement their depleted naval forces. The incipient American government, in response to these provocations, was willing to take on the greatest naval power in the world even though their own navy was critically undermanned.

Long Island Sound, with its bustling shipping industry and deep water harbors, was considered an extremely strategic resource and soon became a prominent target for the powerful British navy. By 1813, British patrols and occasional raids along the Connecticut shoreline prompted the Connecticut Legislature to send two 18-pound cannons and a detachment of militia to protect Stonington Harbor (Wheeler 1900, 61).

During the summer of 1814, as land battles ensued in the southern states and with the British blockade of New London Harbor, few residents in Stonington Borough anticipated an attack on their small town. However, tensions were heightened when an American privateer was pursued into Stonington Harbor by the British after one of their midshipmen, Thomas Powers, was killed during the chase. In retaliation, four British warships anchored off Stonington Point armed with 160 guns and 1275 men poised for attack (de Kay 1990, 1). Knowing that the Stonington militia had been sent to New London, the British commander, Captain Thomas M. Hardy, sent an ultimatum to the town's folk on the evening of 9 August 1814. The ultimatum read:

> Not wishing to destroy the unoffending inhabitants residing in the town of Stonington, one hour is granted them from the receipt of this to remove out of town (Wheeler 1900, 68)

The warning was heeded by many women and children who hastily gathered up what belongings they could carry and fled to the countryside. However, many men stayed behind, alerting the militia in neighboring communities of the British threat, and declaring 'We will defend!' (Wheeler 1900, 69). One young woman, Hulda Hall, was unable to leave as she was tending her dying mother, also named Hulda, who lay failing and unmovable in her bed when the bombardment commenced (Wheeler 1900, 79).

Within an hour, 16 volunteers from Mystic joined the Borough's defenders and, without established military leadership, the militia manned the cannons, returning fire. Evening lit up Stonington Borough like Fourth of July fireworks as the British ships stoked the town with cannonade. The American cannons responded with continual fire until they ran out of powder. Fortunately, the British cannonade ceased around midnight.

If the townspeople thought that the worse was over, they were sadly disappointed when the British fired upon them again at dawn on 10 August. American cannons were helpless until new gunpowder arrived from New London later that morning. After being supplied with gunpowder, the American artillery was able to damage one of the British ships, the HMS *Dispatch*, killing numerous British sailors and forcing the vessel to withdraw from the fighting.

Infuriated, the British resumed the battle with their two remaining ships, HMS *Pactolus* and *Ramillies*. These ships approached the shore in preparation for a more effective bombardment and possible invasion. Under a flag of truce, town leaders rowed out to the *Ramillies*, Captain Hardy's flagship, to negotiate. Why had the British attacked Stonington, they wanted to know? Hardy explained that he believed Stonington was providing torpedoes to the American navy for use against British warships and that the captured wife of the British vice-consul James Stewart was being held prisoner in the town. Captain Hardy demanded that the Americans had until 8 am on the following morning to deliver Mrs Stewart or the entire town would be destroyed (Steenburg 2012).

Mrs Stewart was not being held in Stonington, so there was nothing the town's folk could do but prepare for a further assault, which came at noon on the 11th and continued on and off through the 12th. Finally, on the morning of the 13 August 1814, the British squadron inexplicitly sailed away. The Battle of Stonington was over.

Forty houses were damaged, but none collapsed. Three Americans died during the attack, all from natural causes, not a single death was due to the barrage. On the other side, the British lost 21 men killed, 50 wounded, and HMS *Dispatch* was severely damaged (Palmer 1913). It has been estimated that over 50 tons of metal were spewed into the Borough by British guns, but they clearly sailed away much the worse than this small, maritime port.

According to legend, Hulda Hall had been taking care of her ailing mother in the midst of the assault. When the elderly mother died in her bed (on 10 August 1814), Hulda hurried down to the nearby American battery for assistance in removing and burying her mother. According to Wheeler (1900, 79), a detachment of men, shocked by the young woman's arrival during the bombardment, returned with her to the house where they

> Carefully and tenderly inclosed [*sic*] her remains in the bed and bed-clothes [*sic*] where she lay and bore her to the old Robinson burial place, in the Borough, attended by her daughter. In a deep cut made by the explosion of a bomb-shell [*sic*], without any form of ceremony, except the thunders of the bombardment, they buried her remains.

Another source described that the deceased Hall was carried to the burying ground on her bed, where bed and body were hastily buried in a crater created by one of the exploding British cannonballs. Hulda Hall died in 1830 and was reportedly buried next to her mother in an unmarked grave. As Robinson Burial Grounds was located about 0.5 miles north from their house on Trumbull Street, it is uncertain whether a memorial actually marks the location of the Hall's unmarked graves.

In 1900, a monument was erected in the Robinson Burial Ground by the Children of the American Revolution with the inscription *Hulda Hall heroine of Aug 10, 1814* (Fig. 2.1). This monument is situated in the center of the burial ground (Fig. 2.2). A flat, grassy area with no gravestone evident is located to the immediate north of

Fig. 2.1: Hulda Hall's burial monument in the Robinson Burial Ground, Stonington, Connecticut.

Fig. 2.2: A Web Soil Survey map showing a portion of Stonington Point, the locations of Robinson Burial Ground, and Wadawanuck Square.

this small monument. This open area attracted the attention of local historians and thoughts of possibly containing unmarked graves.

Prior to conducting the GPR investigation, a soil map from the USDA-Natural Resources Conservation Service's Web Soil Survey was reviewed to determine the suitability of soil conditions within the Robinson Burial Ground for GPR. The burial ground is located within a soil delineation that is labeled '29B' (Fig. 2.2). This symbol identifies the soil as Agawam fine sandy loam on 3–8% slopes. The very deep (>1.5 m to bedrock), well drained Agawam soils form in sandy, water deposited material on outwash plains and high stream terraces. These soils consist of a loamy mantle overlying stratified sand and gravel deposits. The loamy mantle ranges from about 40 cm to 90 cm (16–35 in) thick. Water moves rapidly within Agawam soils. Because they commonly lack free water, and have low clay and soluble salt contents, these soils have relatively low electrical conductivities and are considered well suited to GPR. They are also ideal locations for burials as the soils can be easily dug by hand. Agawam soils are considered to have relatively reduced rates of decomposition and therefore have relatively high potential for the preservation of deeply buried bones (Surabian 2012).

To conduct the GPR investigation, a small (5 × 6 m) grid was established across the open area just north of the Huldah Hill monument (Fig. 2.3). Using standard field procedures and a 50 cm grid line interval, 13 parallel traverses were completed in a north–south direction across the grid area with a SIR-3000 control unit. A 400 MHz antenna with an attached survey wheel was used in this survey.

Two representative radar profiles collected from the grid are shown in Figure 2.4. In both profiles, the horizontal distance and the vertical depth scales are expressed in meters. Profile A provides an excellent representation of the Agawam soil. On this profile, a dashed, white line has been used to indicate the inferred contact of the loamy solum with the underlying substratum. The soil solum (A and Bw horizons) appears relatively homogenous and uniformly grey. On this profile, the solum ranges from about 40 cm to 60 cm in depth. One unidentified high amplitude reflection has been indicated by the white arrow. This anomalous feature is presumed to represent either a buried artifact or a displaced stone. In addition, an area of scattered, weak to moderate amplitude reflections is evident within the solum in the first 3.5 m of this radar profile. These reflections suggest an area of soil disturbance. On Figure 2.4, A, the underlying soil substratum (C horizons) consists of smooth to wavy bands of

Fig. 2.3: The GPR grid survey area (bounded by dashed lines) and the Hulda Hall monument (beneath arrow) in the Robinson Burial Ground.

moderate to high amplitude reflections (based on pulse polarity, colored either black or white) suggesting dissimilar strata of sands and gravel. Some of these bands appear to be continuous, while others are broken and consist of shorter segments.

On the radar profile shown in Figure 2.4, B, the near-surface soil materials between the 0.8 m and 3.8 m distance marks contain several small, curved reflection patterns and hyperbolas representing segmented areas of contrasting soil materials and point anomalies embedded in the solum of the Agawam soil. The two white arrows indicate higher amplitude reflections (white and black) from highly contrasting buried point anomalies. As these hyperbolas occur at very shallow (<25 cm) soil depths, they are not believed to represent historical burials but suggest possible buried artifacts, such as covered gravestones. Moving deeper, the contact separating the solum from the underlying substratum has an unexpected and striking 'V' shaped topography. The interior of this feature is nondescript, having only a few low amplitude reflectors. Framing and accentuating the V-shape on each side are higher amplitude, inclined linear reflection patterns. While the identity and origin of the V-shaped feature is unknown, historical accounts and its spatial pattern suggested to the investigators the possibility of a filled bomb crater.

Robinson Burial Ground is located within a block of Wadawanuck Square in present-day downtown Stonington (see Fig. 2.2). During the battle of Stonington, a small band of American volunteers defended the town from a small breastwork that

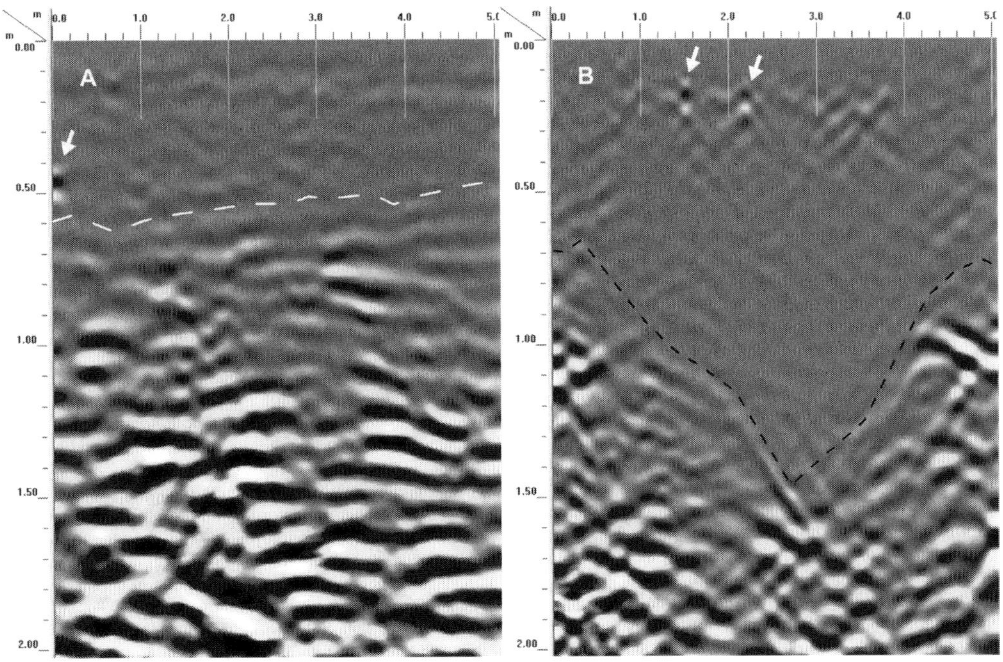

Fig. 2.4: Two representative radar profiles from the GPR survey conducted in the Robinson Burial Ground.

was located further south on Stonington Point, near the breakwater (Haynes 1949). However, according to Haynes, the heaviest concentration of the British cannonade was focused on a Congregational Church steeple that was located near the present-day Wadawanuck Square. The British mistakenly believed that the steeple marked the center of the village. As a consequence, this portion of the village received the heaviest bombardment. It is therefore highly possible that the V-shaped feature shown in Figure 2.4, B represents a refilled bomb crater. This feature appears to be about 4 m at its maximum width and extends to a depth of about 1.5 m.

On Figure 2.4, B there are no reflection patterns that support the presence of skeletal remains or a bed within the suspected refilled bomb crater. Over time, human remains decompose and wooden beds decay. Consequently, as the size of these buried features decreases and the electromagnetic contrast between them and the surrounding soil matrix diminishes, their ability to reflect radar waves will also fade away making them more difficult to locate and interpret with GPR.

After burials, soils will compress and settle above graves. This leads to the placement of additional fill materials to keep the ground surface level. On the radar profile in Figure 2.4, A, there is a weakly expressed layer that extends across the image at a depth of about 10–15 cm. This could be the contact of the A and Bw horizons, or more likely that of redistributed soil materials or fill over the original soil surface. In addition, there is the previously discussed, high amplitude point anomaly and suggestions of a deeper, more extensive area of soil disturbances in the first 3.5 m of the radar profile. Some of these low amplitude reflection patterns have sharp, vertical boundaries and therefore suggest refilled excavations. On Figure 2.4, B there is a noticeable and varied reflection pattern within the upper 40 cm of the soil between the 0.8 m to 3.8 m distance marks. This pattern occurs over the V-shaped feature and is likely an indication of disturbed and contrasting materials and objects.

The collected GPR data from this grid site was further examined using amplitude slice-map analysis. Figure 2.5 contains four time-slice (or depth-slice) amplitude images of the grid area. These depth-slices correspond to estimated soil depths of 0 cm, 50 cm, 100 cm, and 150 cm. For display purposes, each of the depth-slice amplitude images is viewed from directly overhead looking downwards into the grid.

On the four depth-slice images, there is a general increase in the number and amplitude of reflections (high amplitude reflections are colored white) with increasing soil depth. This trend is likely due to the presence of more contrasting strata and inclusions (larger amounts and sizes of rock fragments) in the underlying water deposited materials. On the 50 cm, 100 cm, and 150 cm depth-slice images, a circular area having an absence of higher amplitude reflections is apparent (highlighted within the black dashed partial ellipse). The dimensions of this area appear to decrease with increasing soil depth and correlate well with the V-shaped feature shown on the radar profile in Figure 2.4, B.

On the 100 cm depth-slice image, ten high amplitude (white), linear features have been labeled with dots. Each of these features is elongated in an east–west direction and appear to be at least 1 m in length. As these features provide the best representation of 'grave-like' reflection patterns, they may represent unmarked graves. However, as the underlying stratified sand and gravel deposits also occur at this depth, cautious interpretations are recommended, and some ground-truth excavations are needed to confirm any interpretation prior to identifying these features as unmarked graves.

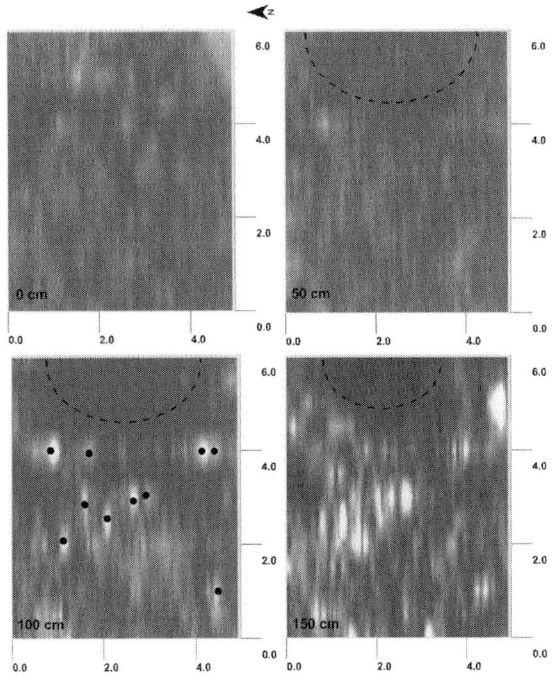

Fig. 2.5: A set of four depth-slice amplitude images created from the GPR data collected at the Robinson Burial Ground.

At this site, while interpretations are unconfirmed, the use of GPR showed a subsurface structure that fits historical accounts of the British bombardment of this portion of Stonington. While other interpretations are possible, images from the GPR survey suggest the likelihood of a bomb hitting and exploding within the Robinson Burial Ground. Not fully substantiated by GPR was the historical record of the woman hastily buried in her bed in the crater. Reading historical accounts about the burial and number of bombs that hit the area and knowing GPR could not verify a burial within the bomb crater, some ambiguity still exists about exactly where the women may be buried. Without digging in this suspected bomb crater at the Robinson Burial Ground, investigators will never know, but the story can continue.

Chapter 3

A Revolutionary War mass burial, Old Norwichtown Burying Ground, Norwich

The Old Norwichtown Burying Ground (also referred to as the Colonial Cemetery) is located on Old Cemetery Lane in the Historic District of Norwichtown, Connecticut. This district, which includes much of the town's original settlement area, is listed on the National Register of Historic Places. The burying ground was established in 1700 near the town green and contains, most notably, the graves of Samuel Huntington, a signer of the Declaration of Independence; several Revolutionary War leaders and soldiers; as well as Hannah Arnold, the mother of Benedict Arnold, the Revolutionary military hero who infamously defected to the British army. The burying ground is also reputed to be the burial place for 20 Frenchmen who died from diseases during the American Revolution. In an historical account of Norwich, Connecticut, Frances Caulkins (1845, 237), wrote:

> In 1778, a body of French troops, on the route from Providence to the south, halted there [Norwichtown] for ten or fifteen days, on account of sickness among them. They had their tents spread upon the plain [Norwichtown Green], while the sick were quartered in the court house. About twenty died and were buried each side of the lane that led into the old burying yard [Old Norwichtown Burying Ground]. No stones were set up, and the ground was soon smoothed over so as to leave no trace of the narrow tenements below.

Based on Caulkins' account, in 1901, a stone boulder with an attached bronze plaque was erected by the Daughters of the American Revolution (DAR) in the area she described (Fig. 3.1). It reads:

In Memory of
Twenty French Soldiers
Who, Under Lafayette,
Died While In Camp at
Norwich Town 1778

Fig. 3.1: The boulder placed by the Daughters of the American Revolution as a memorial to the 20 Frenchmen buried near the entrance to the Old Norwichtown Burying Ground.

However, there are no extant primary historic documents suggesting that the Marquis de Lafayette marched through Connecticut in 1778, much less that 20 'sick' French soldiers died in Norwich. It would not be until late 1780 that the French allied with America in its effort to overthrow British colonial rule and Brigadier Duc de Luazun's cavalry would encamp in nearby Lebanon (Stevenson 1923, 299). To complicate the story, the French Historical Society in the 1920s erected a second monument behind the DAR's memorial to honor their fallen ancestors (Fig. 3.2). It reads translated into English:

In Memory
Twenty Companions of Lafayette
Who died for American Liberty,
At the Town of Norwich
Pious Guardians of French Remembrance:

Was the second monument simply a repetition of unsubstantiated historical information? We all love a history mystery, but the City of Norwich wanted to know if there really was such a mass grave at the burying ground.

Fig. 3.2: The monument donated by the French Historical Society and placed uphill from the DAR commemorative boulder.

We do know that smallpox, yellow fever, and other communicable diseases ravished American, French, and British forces during the Revolutionary War. The magnitude of smallpox impacting the Continental Army was significant, especially in the early years of the war, when it influenced military strategies. Smallpox affected recruitment, increased desertions, weakened the fighting force, and was so virulent that the British were rumored to have used the virus as a biological weapon during George Washington's siege of Boston in 1776 (Becker 2004, 381). The situation was so serious that Washington reluctantly made the controversial decision to inoculate his troops, which, in the end, probably saved his army (Becker 2004, 430).

One of the places where smallpox acutely ravished Patriot soldiers was aboard prison ships anchored in British-controlled New York Harbor. Vessels like the HMS *Jersey* were repurposed from warships to prison pens. These vessels became hellholes from which Revolutionary War prisoners of war (POW) were confined below decks in crowded, nauseous conditions that were ripe for the spread of smallpox and other communicable diseases. Doomed American and French prisoners were often sick, fed rotted food, drank contaminated water, suffered infestations of lice, and had to endure suffocating heat and frigid cold. They sadly died in considerable numbers even as smallpox threatened their British captors.

On New Year's Eve 1776, the British, fearing the spread of smallpox from 200 incarcerated, infirmed captives sailed one of their prison ships out of New York and into Long Island Sound to Milford, Connecticut. There on the first day of 1777, they dumped their infected prisoners onto the beach leaving the locals to tend to the dying. One Milford resident, Capt Steven Stow, would personally care for the ailing soldiers. Regrettably, he and 46 of the former prisoners died and were buried in a mass grave at Milford Center Cemetery.

What of the purported mass burial in Old Norwichtown Burying Ground? Based on research recently conducted by Norwich City Historian, Dale Plummer (2020), three pieces of evidence have surfaced that may shed some light on the mysterious French soldiers. First, an article from the 12 October 1778 edition of *The Norwich Packet* states:

> Last Saturday arrived in this town from Boston, under a proper guard, and this day set out for New York, about 230 British prisoners, taken by the Count d'Estaing's; they are to be exchanged for the like number of Frenchmen, captured by the English. (Cregeau 2020)

Secondly, Plummer found a letter from Norwich resident Brigadier General Jedediah Huntington to his father dated 25 October 1778, stating that

> between 5 and 600 Frenchmen came in from New York ... they arrived here last Night. Part are gone on this day to Boston. (Huntington 1923, 31)

Thirdly, on November 21, 1778, the Rev. Benjamin Lord gave a sermon providing some demographic statistics pertinent to his Norwich congregation:

> Baptisms this year, 40. Deaths, 36. Of those, infants, 5. Children from 2 years, with the youth to 25, are 10. From the age of 25 to 50, are 13. From 50 to 94, are 7. *And also died here in a few weeks, of the French from New-York, 20* [authors' italics]. In all, 56. (Lord 1778, 31)

This seems to all but solve our mystery: the 20 French soldiers were prisoners of war being exchanged by British for some of their own soldiers captured by the French and Americans. Suffering from smallpox, they died and were buried in the local cemetery. Well, maybe not. According to Plummer (2020), they could have been French sailors impressed by the British Navy and not infantry. Nonetheless, sailors or soldiers, thanks to Dale Plummer's research, we have primary historical context for the French deaths. But is there any evidence of a mass grave beneath the grass-covered entryway that leads into the burying ground?

Based on the aforementioned account given by Frances M. Caulkins (1845), an 11 × 25 m grid was established along the grass-covered entryway that leads into the Old Norwichtown Burying Ground and the adjoining slope (Figs 3.3 and 3.4), in an attempt to locate these unmarked graves with GPR. The survey was completed using the SIR-4000 data acquisition system with a 400 MHz antenna; both attached to a survey cart that was equipped with an odometer wheel. A total of 23, 25 m long radar traverses, spaced 50 cm apart, were conducted in a west to east direction across this

Fig. 3.3: The GPR grid site along the entryway to the burying ground. The left hand arrow identifies the French Historical Society monument and the right hand arrow points towards the DAR commemorative boulder.

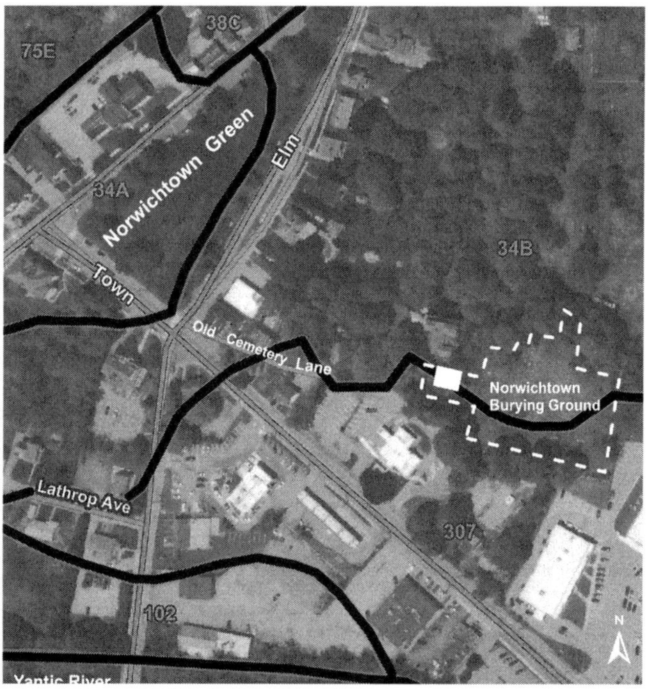

Fig. 3.4: This Web Soil Survey map shows the soils mapped in the area surrounding the Old Norwichtown Burying Ground. The approximate boundaries of this burying ground have been outlined with white dashed lines. The white rectangle indicates the approximate location of the GPR survey grid.

grid area. Radar profiles collected along these traverse (grid) lines were submitted to standard processing procedures of time-zero correction and background removal, with suitable color table and transform selections. The average velocity of pulse propagation and the depth scale were estimated by hyperbola matching.

A Web Soil Survey map of the burying ground (white dashed line) is shown in Figure 3.4. On this map, the location of the GPR grid site within the boundary of the burying ground is identified by the white rectangle. The soil survey map shows that the grid was located along a boundary line that separates two soil delineations: Merrimac fine sandy loam on 3–8% slopes (34B); and Urban land (307). The very deep (>1.5 m to bedrock), somewhat excessively drained, Merrimac soils form principally in outwash deposits. The solum (A and Bw horizons) of Merrimac soils typically ranges from about 45 cm to 90 cm (18–37 in) thick and consists mostly of aeolian deposits with minor inclusions of rock fragments as a result of soil mixing processes (e.g., frost action, tree throw, and animal burrowing). The solum is underlain by the substratum, which consists of contrasting layers of outwash composed of sands, gravels, and cobbles. Because the outwash contrasts with the solum in terms of soil texture, bulk density, number of rock fragments, and moisture content, the boundary that separates them is typically distinct. As a consequence, the solum/substratum interface produces a noticeable reflection pattern on most GPR radar profiles. However, these reflections will vary in amplitude depending upon variations in the abruptness and contrast of soil properties across this boundary. Merrimac soils are considered well suited for deep profiling with GPR and to afford relatively reduced rates of decomposition. They therefore have relatively high potential for the preservation of deeply buried bones (Surabian 2012). Urban land is defined as land that is covered by pavement, buildings and other, impervious, human-manufactured surfaces and structures. Underlying these impermeable layers and structures, artificially altered or transported earthen materials, natural soil materials, or a mix of both can occur. As evident in Figure 3.3, the area of Urban land includes the stone wall and parking lot to the right (south) of the grid site.

Figure 3.5 is a 2D radar profile from the traverse that passed closest to the 1901 DAR commemorative boulder. On this radar profile, the commemorative boulder is located near the 7.0 m distance mark. Within the upper 10–15 cm of this profile, the continuous reflection bands represent the surface layer that consists of fill and/or slope-washed materials. In the upper 10–50 cm of this profile, the inserted black, undulating dashed line represents a weakly expressed interface, which is presumed to represent the contact of fill and/or slope-washed materials with the underlying soil solum. Because of the increasing number of point reflectors with increasing depth and the presence of a transitional layer (BC horizon) that contains gravels and cobbles, the contact of the solum with the underlying substratum is weakly expressed or obscured on this profile.

On the radar profile shown in Figure 3.5, two fairly conspicuous sets of higher amplitude, horizontal reflection bands can be seen at a depth of about 30 cm near the 5.0 m and 8.5 m distance marks (see black arrows). Each set is over 1 m in length. Though their identities are unknown, these reflectors could represent the remnants of

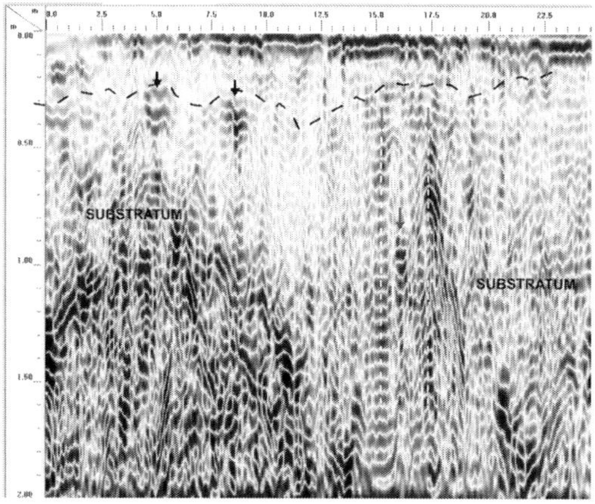

Fig. 3.5: Radar profile from the traverse that was collected nearest to the DAR commemorative boulder.

shallow burials or buried grave markers. Below the 15 m and 17.5 m distance marks, at a depth of about 50 cm, two reflection hyperbolas (indicated by grey arrows) are apparent. These reflectors are believed to represent a burial associated with a gravestone (see Fig. 3.3, next to the large tree in the near-center background). The two underlying, white, dashed, vertical lines have been inserted to highlight reverberated reflection patterns. These reverberated or 'ringing' patterns suggest the probability that the two reflection hyperbolas represent more highly reflective, buried metallic objects. A dark grey arrow has been used to highlight an anomalous feature that is located between these two reverberating reflection patterns at a depth of about 90 cm. This anomalous feature could represent a burial.

The two radar profiles shown in Figure 3.6 are from adjoining traverse lines that were collected along the centerline of the entryway into the burying ground (see Fig. 3.3). On the upper radar profile, the reverberating, moderate amplitude reflector (highlighted by black arrow) represents a buried metallic object. On both radar profiles, the continuous, slightly inclined near-surface layer (see black dashed lines) is interpreted as the original surface layer that has been buried beneath layers of fill and/or slope-washed materials. As noted by Frances Caulkins (1845), the surface of the lane into the burying yard had been 'smoothed over' [probably with fill materials added to level the surface]. The boundary separating the soil solum from the underlying outwash deposits, though weakly expressed and partially masked by point reflectors, is interpreted to range in depth from about 50–100 cm. Though difficult to trace laterally, the presence of this boundary can be inferred by subtle to intense variations in the number, size, arrangement, and amplitude of reflections.

On each of the radar profiles shown in Figure 3.6, an area between the 1 m and 15 m distance marks has been highlighted by the black, segmented lines of a rounded rectangle. The enclosed subsurface area contains a noticeable clustering of multiple, high amplitude reflection hyperbolas, which contrasts and sets this portion of the substratum apart from the portion between the 15 m and 25 m distance marks. As these radar profiles were collected along the old lane or entryway into the burying ground, this contrasting pattern of multiple, closely spaced reflection hyperbolas may represent the burials of the 20 French soldiers that were noted by Frances Caulkins (1845). However, the high amplitudes of these reflection patterns are a source of interest and uncertainty. The graves were interred over 300 years ago.

While it is not known how they were buried, with the passage of time, wooden coffins and shroud-wrapped interments disintegrate and will become less contrasting with the enveloping soil matrix. Although Merrimac soils have a high potential for bone preservation, bones are generally too small and lack sufficient contrast with the surrounding soil matrix to be detected with GPR. In light of these specifics, it is equally possible that the high amplitude reflection hyperbolas represent a clustering of rock fragments and/or contrasting strata or inhomogeneities within the outwash.

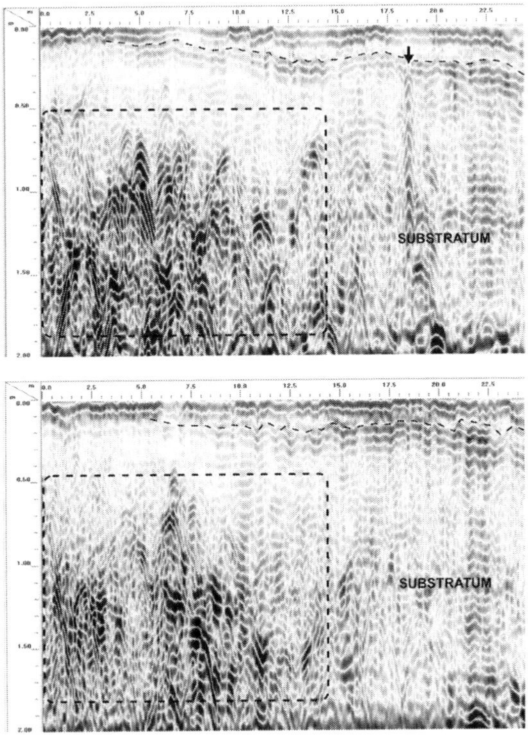

Fig. 3.6: Two consecutive radar profiles that were collected near and parallel with the centerline of the entryway into the Old Norwichtown Burying Ground.

Figure 3.7 presents three depth-slice images from the grid site. These images show the spatial reflection patterns at depths of 30 cm, 80 cm, and 130 cm. On the 30 cm depth-slice image, the two high amplitude reflectors that were noted on the radar profile in Figure 3.5 have been identified with black arrows. These two reflection patterns stand out on this depth-slice image. Though short, they do appear to be 'grave-like'. However, their long axes extend in a north–south direction, which would be atypically of the customary, east-facing orientation of burials at that time, but similar to other patterns appearing in the western (right hand) portion of the grid site. On the 80 cm and 130 cm depth-slice images, white arrows have been used to identify the anomalous, closely spaced reflectors that were noted on the radar profile in Figure 3.5. These reflection anomalies are believed to represent a burial associated with the gravestone near the tree visible on Figure 3.3.

On the three depth-slice images shown in Figure 3.7, the old lane or entryway to the burying ground extends across the grid area along its southern boundary. The number of randomly spaced, high amplitude (white) reflections increase with depth on these three images. Some of these reflections appear aligned forming linear, north–south patterns. The eastern (left hand) and western (right hand) halves of the solum (30 cm depth-slice image) are distinct, based on the number of reflectors. The eastern half appears comparatively free of reflectors, while the western half contains a larger number of reflectors with many appearing to have their long axes

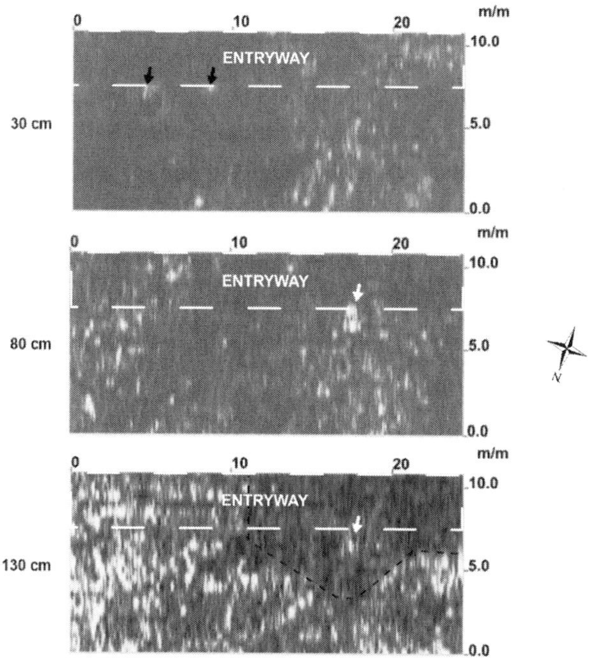

Fig. 3.7: These three depth-slice amplitude images are from soil depths of 30 cm, 80 cm, and 130 cm.

orientated in a north–south direction. Near the contact of the solum with the underlying substratum (80 cm depth-slice image), the number of reflectors increases, most noticeably in the extreme south-eastern and north-western portions of the grid.

Except for the south-west quadrant of the grid, the substratum (130 cm depth-slice image) contains the greatest number and density of high amplitude reflectors. On this depth-slice image, the eastern 10 m portion of the burying ground's entryway (located along upper border of this image) is more densely covered by point and linear reflection patterns than the western portion. Rather than being randomly distributed, the reflection patterns in the eastern portion of the entryway appear to be arranged in two distinct rows, each consisting of closely spaced, north–south orientated, linear reflectors. These patterns attract attention as they have the appearance and suggest the potential for the location of the mass grave. A distinct area composed of lower amplitude reflection patterns appears in the south-west portion of the 130 cm depth-slice image. This area contrasts noticeably with other portions of this image. The boundary separating these two areas appears abrupt and highly contrasting. As these two areas are distinct and noticeable, they are suspected to have different compositions and may warrant further in-depth investigations.

The GPR survey of the Old Norwichtown Burying Ground, while providing insight into subsurface conditions, was inconclusive in confirming the exact locations of the 20 Frenchmen that were reportedly buried here. While the soils are highly suited to deep and high resolution profiling with GPR, their complex composition and structure obscured the clarity and accuracy of identifying potential gravesites. Radar profiles and depth-slice imagery revealed the presence of several reflection hyperbolas and patterns that could potentially represent burials, but a high degree of uncertainty is attached to these interpretations based on the known composition and structure of the underlying glacial outwash. The composition and structure of the outwash creates reflection inhomogeneities and scattering bodies that obscured the identification of the remnants of burials. The GPR survey did, however, reveal the locations of several anomalous features whose reflection patterns and locations suggest burials or possible remnants of graves. Computer processing and imaging of the radar profiles distinguished two distinct areas along the entryway that had noticeably different reflection patterns and presumably different compositions and/or structures. Discernibly, the eastern portion of the entryway exhibited reflection patterns that suggested the potential for a mass grave.

Chapter 4

The unmarked grave of Jeff Liberty, African-American Revolutionary War Veteran, Old Judea Cemetery, Washington

It was an offer he had yearned for, hardly dared to hope for, and was relieved to receive. Jonathan Farrand, a Captain in the Continental Army, proffered his 55 year-old African captive, Jeff, the longed-for proposition: serve as a fighting soldier in this War of Rebellion against England and I will grant your freedom. Though well past middle age, Jeff eagerly consented taking on the surname, 'Liberty' acknowledging his personal emancipation and espousing the concept he and other African-American soldiers were fighting for. For a man who had spent a life in bondage it has a sound of irony.

Jeff Liberty's military service commenced in the summer of 1781 when he entered the all-Black Second Company of the Fourth Connecticut Regiment. Every officer, commissioned and non-commissioned, was White; all the privates were Black. Interestingly, there were over 40 other African Americans serving in various Connecticut regiments that could have collectively formed a second all-Black company but instead remained in their integrated units (White 1973, 18).

When the Revolutionary War began in 1775 with the firing of armaments at Concord and Lexington, Massachusetts, freed Black people and captives responded to the call for troops, however, there was concern by the military and private property owners that those enslaved would use the excuse of joining the army as a means of running away and feared that arming slaves could cause an insurrection (White 1973). Even George Washington decided to exclude Black people from serving in the Continental Army in 1775 to the unanimous approval of all his officers. However, by the end of 1777, the war situation had deteriorated with the British taking control of New York and the Continental Army having increasing troubles recruiting men to fight. As a consequence, freed Blacks and those enslaved were being actively recruited in many states.

Slaves were motivated to enlist in the army for a number of reasons, but the primary incentive was the promise of emancipation by their owners at the end of the war. Many were used as replacements to fill quotas for the Continental Army that many towns found hard to achieve, while others fought in place of their masters. There is no record as to how many slaves received their freedom by the end of the war (Moore 1862, 6–7).

Jonathan Ferrand's large farm was snuggled into the hummocks of Judea Parish, the east region of the Town of Washington, in Connecticut's Litchfield Hills. Jonathan was born in Milford, Connecticut, in 1728, but moved as a youth to the farming community of Washington. When the Revolutionary War broke out he enlisted as a Lieutenant and was soon promoted to Captain in Colonel Increase Moseley's Regiment. After the war he continued to rise in prominence among the town's citizens when they elected him as State Representative for their District. He also operated a tollgate at his residence along the Woodbury Turnpike, an important road connecting the river port of Derby at the confluence of the Housatonic and Naugatuck Rivers to the state's north-west corner. He owned seven African Americans: Caesar, Jeff and his wife, Phyllis, and four others (Moore 1862, 6–7).

Unfortunately, we know little about Jeff Liberty and his family other than he survived the War of Independence and returned to his home in Washington where he lived with his wife and two daughters in an area then known as 'under the hill'. Here, Jeff Liberty farmed a small piece of land that was given to him for his military service. He died in 1797 at the age of 72 and was buried in Old Judea Cemetery, which was located on the hill just upslope from his farm.

Today, by the entrance to the Old Judea Cemetery, is a stone memorial that was raised in 1998 by the Judea Chapter of the Connecticut Daughters of the American Revolution commemorating 34 soldiers of the War for Independence who are buried within the cemetery (Fig. 4.1). All the burial sites of the White soldiers

Fig. 4.1: The memorial at the entrance to the Old Judea Cemetery listing the names of the provincial soldiers who served in the American Revolutionary War (1775–1783) and are buried within the cemetery. Jeff Liberty's name is listed on the top right-side of the marker.

Fig. 4.2: The GPR grid site in the Old Judea Cemetery. The American flag is believed to mark the grave site of Jeff Liberty.

have engraved headstones, however, there is one veteran's gravesite that remained unmarked – Jeffrey Liberty. If his burial was originally marked in any manner, it had been lost over time. In the 1920s, in remembrance of this individual and his service to this country, the Connecticut Society of the Sons of the American Revolution erected a small iron marker over an area that was assumed to be his burial site. It is engraved *Jeff Liberty And His Colored Patriots* (see Fig. 4.6 below).

To provide a more fitting memorial for Jeff Liberty and his wife, the Sons of the American Revolution purchased a gravestone to place over his gravesite to replace the wooden stake and American flag (the iron marker had been removed to prevent its theft) that had commemorated what was believed to be their resting place (Fig. 4.2). However, as it is common knowledge that grave markers do not always reflect the actual position of burials (Fiedler *et al.* 2009; Doolittle and Bellantoni 2010), a GPR survey was requested to help confirm burials near the wooden stake and American flag which may be the location of Jeff Liberty's gravesite.

A Web Soil Survey map showing the Old Judea Cemetery (Fig. 4.3) reveals that the suspected site of Jeff Liberty's grave is located within a soil delineation that is labeled '38C'. This symbol identifies the soil map unit as Hinckley loamy sand on 3–15% slopes. The very deep (>1.5 m to bedrock), excessively drained Hinckley soils formed in glaciofluvial sands and gravels. These soils consist of a loamy sand mantle overlying stratified sand and gravel deposits. The mantle ranges from about 30 cm to 87 cm (12–34 in) thick. Water moves rapidly through these soils. Because Hinckley soils commonly lack free water, have low clay and soluble salt contents, and therefore low electrical conductivities, they are considered well suited to GPR. However, the substratum of Hinckley soils contains rock fragments whose reflections on radar imagery can produce high levels of unwanted noise and clutter, which can obscure reflections from desired archaeological targets, foster uncertainties, and restrain interpretations. Hinckley soils are considered to have moderate potential for the preservation of deeply buried bones, wooden caskets, and other perishable features (Surabian 2012).

A 10 × 11 m grid was established across an open, grass covered area that included the wooden stake and American flag (white square on Fig. 4.3). A total of 21, 11 m long radar traverses, each spaced 50 cm apart, were completed from north to south across this grid. In addition, several random GPR traverses were also completed in the area surrounding the stake and flag.

The survey was completed using an SIR-4000 radar unit and a 400 MHz antenna, both attached to a survey cart that was equipped with an odometer wheel. The collected radar profiles were submitted to time-zero correction and background

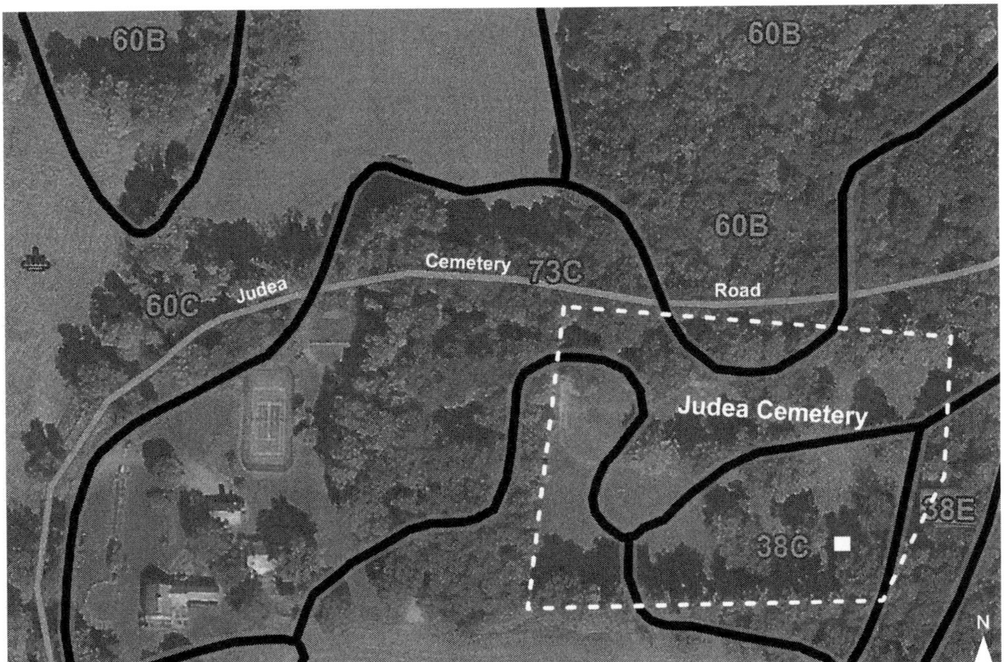

Fig. 4.3: A Web Soil Survey map showing the area surrounding the Old Judea Cemetery. The approximate boundaries of this cemetery have been outlined with white dashed lines. The white rectangle indicates the approximate location of where the GPR grid survey was completed.

removal processing procedures. Suitable color table and transform selections were made to examine and display the collected radar imagery. The average velocity of pulse propagation and the depth scale were estimated by hyperbola matching.

The three radar profiles shown in Figure 4.4 are from traverses that were conducted across the grid site from north to south. These profiles are labeled and arranged according to the distance from the north-east corner of the grid. On each profile, the horizontal distance (top distance marks in meters) is measured from north to south. All measurements are expressed in meters. The radar profile labeled Line 3.0 m passed closest to the wooden stake and flag.

In terms of profiling depths, resolution of subsurface features, and structures shown, these radar images are considered representative of Hinckley soils. The surface reflection appears as linear bands of low to moderate amplitudes. The solum (A and Bw horizons) appears to range in depth from about 40 cm to 70 cm. Where undisturbed, the solum appears white to light gray in color and lacks distinguishing features. The contact of the solum with the underlying substratum is partially obscured by higher amplitude point reflectors. The underlying substratum (C horizons) consists of inclined, wavy to contorted bands of weak to moderate amplitude linear reflections (light gray to black), which suggest contrasting layers of outwash materials that were deposited in a turbulent environment.

In each of the radar profiles shown in Figure 4.4, black arrows have been used to identify observable, higher amplitude reflection hyperbola in the solum. As these occur within depths of less than 50 cm, they are believed to be too shallow to represent burials and are interpreted as representing point reflectors such as larger tree roots or rock fragments.

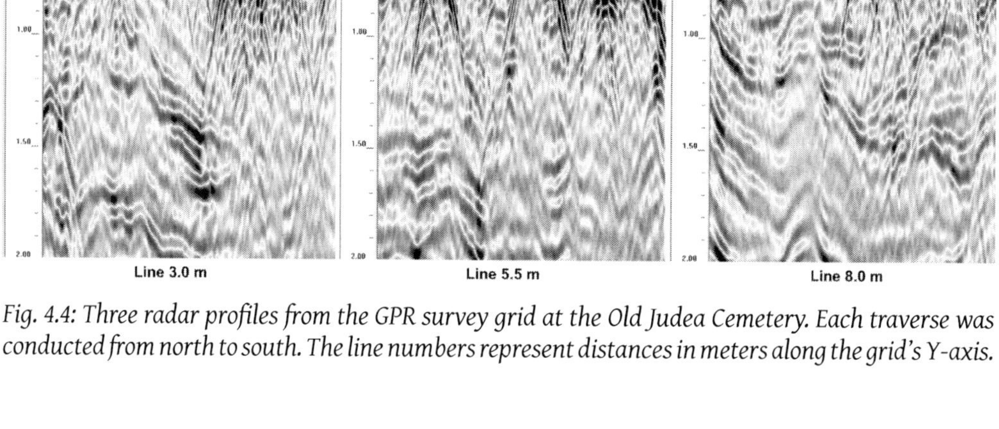

Fig. 4.4: Three radar profiles from the GPR survey grid at the Old Judea Cemetery. Each traverse was conducted from north to south. The line numbers represent distances in meters along the grid's Y-axis.

In each profile, a weakly expressed area of apparent soil disturbance has been indicated by a segmented, horizontal line with arrows at each end. These areas of suspected soil disturbance have contrasting reflection patterns and slightly higher reflection amplitudes than adjoining areas of the soil solum. These shallow to moderately deep disturbance signatures could represent depressions formed by potential grave shafts that have been filled with mixed and contrasting soil materials. With the passage of time, natural soil-forming processes erase the signs of disturbance and reduce the contrast in dielectric properties, which can account for the variability in expression and the low amplitudes of these reflection patterns on the three radar profiles. In the upper 20–30 cm of the disturbance signatures identified on the 3.0 m and 5.5 m line traverses, weakly expressed, slightly concave-upward or 'bowl-like' signatures are apparent. These patterns have been associated with the settling of soil materials used to fill the grave shafts and the accumulation of added soil materials used to level the surface (Doolittle and Bellantoni 2010).

On each of the profiles shown in Figure 4.4, elongated, grey arrows have been used to identify vertical patterns of lower amplitude reflections that suggest potential grave shafts. As noted by Leach (2021), differences in soil moisture contents and the structure of the backfill materials may be sufficient to generate contrasts in dielectric properties with the surrounding soil matrix, thus making the grave shaft visible. In these instances, the grave shaft, if apparent, will have a low amplitude and can be easily overlooked (Leach 2021).

Black chevrons have been inserted on these radar profiles over high amplitude reflection patterns that occur along the contact of the solum with the underlying substratum. These reflection patterns are larger, and more intense and irregularly-shaped than the overlying point reflectors that are assumed to represent tree roots. Though these features occur at shallow depth (40–70 cm) and along a major soil structural contact, the idea that they represent burials cannot be ruled out. On the radar profile for Line 8.0 m, the letter 'A' has been inserted over a smeared, convex-upwards, low amplitude reflection pattern of unknown origins. This peculiar vertical pattern spans the entire depth of this profile. A fitting interpretation for this feature remains problematic.

The GPR data that was collected from the grid site was examined using amplitude slice-map analysis. Figure 4.5 contains four time-slice (or depth-slice) amplitude images of the grid. These four depth-slices provide planar views of the soil at projected depths of 25 cm, 50 cm, 75 cm, and 100 cm. For display purposes, each of the depth-slice amplitude images is viewed from directly overhead looking downwards into the grid. On each depth-slice image, a black dot marks the alleged site of Jeff Liberty's grave.

On the depth-slice images shown in Figure 4.5 there are a greater number and concentration of higher amplitude (black and dark grey) reflection patterns in the south-east portion (upper left) of the grid. In other portions, the reflection patterns appear more sporadic, less continuous, and of lower reflection amplitudes. While some

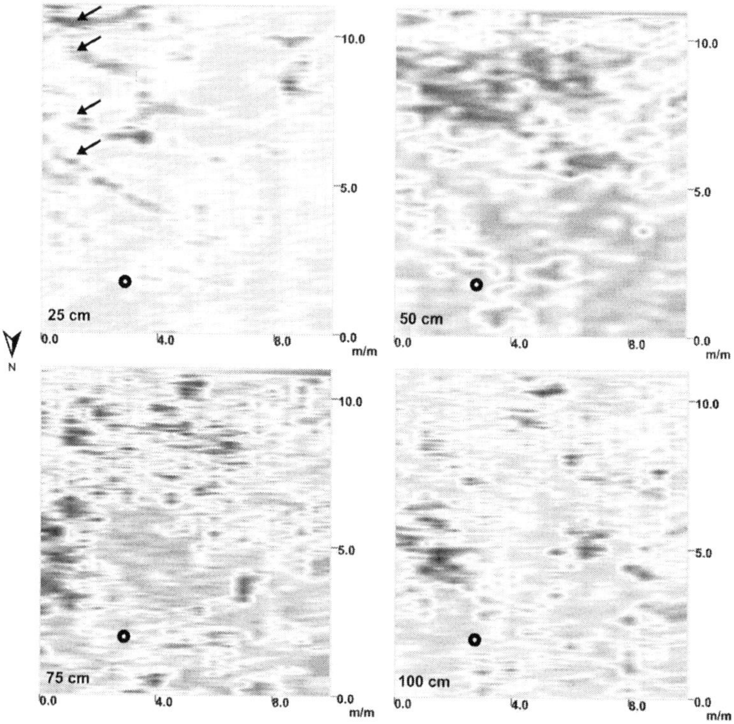

Fig. 4.5: Four depth-slice amplitude images from the GPR grid. The partially filled, black dot represents the location of the American flag and wooden stake that were assumed to be the site of Jeff Liberty's grave.

reflection patterns appear to have 'grave-like' shapes, none clearly stands out and can be confidently interpreted as representing a grave.

On the 25 cm depth-slice image, several higher amplitude, linear reflection patterns (identified with black arrows) appear to stretch in a north-westerly direction from the east side into the middle portion of the grid. These features are believed to represent reflections from larger roots linked to a tree located near the south-east corner of the grid (see Fig. 4.2). Reflection hyperbolas from these roots were noted on the radar profiles in Figure 4.4. With the exception of some moderate to high amplitude linear reflection patterns in the south-west (upper right hand) corner of the grid, the remainder of the 25 cm depth-slice image is devoid of any significant reflection patterns, the lack of which was anticipated based on the characteristics of the Hinkley soil.

On the 50 cm depth-slice image, a noticeable area of higher amplitude reflections is evident in the southern part (upper portion) of the grid. These reflections form a broad linear pattern that appears elongated in an east to west direction. A second linear pattern branches off from this pattern in a north-westerly direction. Within these two broad patterns, several grave-like shapes can be visualized, but none can be so identified with any degree of certainty. In addition, on the 50 cm, 75 cm, and 100 cm depth-slice amplitude images, though more subdued and consisting of lower amplitude reflections, similar (south-east to north-west orientation) patterns are present across the entire grid area. Though varying in expression, the consistent orientation of these patterns suggests alternating strata of outwash materials. The decrease in their reflection amplitudes with depth is partially attributed to increasing signal scattering losses and attenuation.

On the 75 cm and 100 cm depth-slice amplitude images, multiple, rectangular-shaped reflection patterns that are elongated in an east to west direction are scattered across the grid area. The shape of many of these features appears 'grave-like' and suggest potential burials. However, uncertainties exist as inhomogeneities in the substratum cannot be ruled out.

Fig. 4.6: The new headstone for Jeff Liberty and his wife, Phyllis Liberty, erected in the Old Judea Cemetery. The iron marker, erected by the Connecticut Sons of the American Revolution in the 1920s, is engraved JEFF LIBERTY AND HIS COLORED PATRIOTS.

Depth-slice amplitude images of the grid site revealed only weak and poorly defined reflection patterns near the American flag and wooden stake that were believed to be the location of Jeff and Phyllis Liberty's burials. Although some 'grave-like' reflection patterns could be envisioned throughout the 10 × 11 m grid site, all lacked acceptable clarity on the depth-slice images. As a consequence, interpretations of the depth-slice images were considered unreliable. However, several anomalous reflection patterns that are suggestive of potential burials appeared on many of the radar profiles collected across this grid site. With a higher degree of confidence, these reflection patterns were associated with unmarked graves. Based on these interpretations, the grid area is believed to contain a number of unmarked graves, one of which is located near the American flag and wooden stake.

Based on these finding, without any excavations, and to bring a long overdue honor to this war soldier, the Gov. Wolcott Branch #10, Connecticut Sons of the American Revolution purchased a headstone to mark the gravesites of Jeff and Phyllis Liberty (Fig. 4.6). At a graveside ceremony on 19 October 2019, this Patriot and former slave was venerated in speech and memory with an engraved headstone like other Revolutionary War veterans interred in the Old Judea Cemetery.

Chapter 5

The Starr family's hidden tomb, North Burying Ground, Danbury

'Who was Dr. Jabes Starr?' That question was on everyone's mind when his name appeared, chiseled across the exposed face of a polished white marble doorway at the entrance of a rediscovered bygone tomb; even the city historian had never heard of him.

A 5 ft by 7 inch (*c.* 152 × 13 cm) rectangular concrete slab had, for many years, been exposed along the upper edge of a south-facing hill slope within the North Burying Ground (also known as North Main Street Cemetery, Old North Main Street Cemetery, Old Main Street Cemetery) in Danbury, Connecticut. Local historians had long been curious as to the presence and purpose of this undecorated piece of concrete protruding from their manicured lawn, especially since cemetery records and plot maps do not exist concerning graves in this section of the burying ground. By 2014, progressive erosion began exposing red-fired bricks along the edge of this slab suggesting the potential for a buried structure, possibly an underground tomb. The Connecticut State Archaeologist was consulted and, with permission from the City of Danbury, agreed to conduct a minor excavation at the site for the purposes of uncovering the structure's façade to determine its function.

During this preliminary archaeological investigation, soil materials downslope from the slab were systematically removed exposing the top of a marble door to a buried vault (Fig. 5.1, A), which had not only been deliberately covered and concealed but also had been barricaded with a mortared brick wall. Whoever enclosed the vault from sight meant for no-one to ever re-open it. As the excavation extended deeper, with additional soil and bricks removed, a marble stone doorway with two long historical-era rusted iron hinges was exposed. These hinges stretched two-thirds across the marble gate and were immovable due to corrosion. On the face of the marble door to the vault (Fig. 5.1, B), an engraved inscription was revealed:

Dr. Jabes Starr's
Family Vault, 1804

This newly discovered family name sent Robert 'Bob' Young of the Danbury Museum and Historical Society into their archives. Research revealed that Dr Jabez Starr (1755–1840) was a prominent supporter of the American Revolution, a practicing physician, and a tavern owner, though little else about him appeared in Danbury's historical records. We do know that he was born about 1755 and married Mary Elliot, the daughter of John and Dorcas (Holmes) Elliot, who was a native of nearby Bedford, New York, just across the Connecticut state line. Dr Starr died in February 1840. There was no information about the family vault at North Burying Ground and no extant burial records identifying the family members entombed. The tomb appears to have been deliberately covered with earth to conceal its location and visibility.

The Starr Family Genealogy (Starr 1879) indicates that Jabes and Mary had three children that survived infancy: Elizabeth, born in 1780; Lewis, b. 1782; and, Levi, b. 1783. They had a number of other children who died in infancy, including a daughter, Mariah, in 1804 – the date on the tomb! We surmised that, Dr Starr had the vault built for the interment of her remains and those of family members to follow.

Fig. 5.1: A. The excavated and exposed marble door to the unrecorded vault in the North Burying Ground, Danbury, Connecticut; B. the inscription engraved on the marble door reads 'Dr. Jabez Starr's Family Vault, 1804'.

As the graves for Dr Starr, his wife, his two sons, and his daughter are not recorded in this cemetery's records, it is believed that they may also have been interred in the vault along with Mariah. While the reason why this vault was concealed remains a mystery, it must have occurred prior to 1930 when a detailed record of all vaults and headstones in the state of Connecticut was compiled (Hale Index 1935). However, in this record, there is no mention of the Starr Family Tomb.

Following this preliminary archaeological investigation, the State Archaeologist recommended that a reconnaissance GPR survey be conducted over the buried vault to estimate its areal extent and dimensions. Before conducting the survey, the identity, characteristics, and suitability for GPR of the soils surrounding the buried vault were reviewed. A soil survey map that includes the North Burying Ground is shown in Figure 5.2. The vault is located in a soil delineation that is labelled '84D', which signifies an area of Paxton and Montauk fine sandy loam on 15–25% slopes. The well drained, very deep (>1.5 m to bedrock) Paxton and Montauk soils formed in lodgment tills, which consist of unsorted glacial drift deposited beneath a glacier. In areas of Paxton and Montauk soils, the depth to this compacted layer (Cd horizon) ranges from about 50 cm to 100 cm (20–40 in). Water will briefly perch on this contact during wetter periods. However, the depth to the water table in these soils is greater than 2 m (6.6 ft), even under wet conditions. Because of their low clay, water, and soluble salt contents, Paxton and Montauk soils are considered well suited to GPR applications but because of the presence of a compacted layer, which restricts the movement of soil water, and acidic soil reactions, these soils are considered to have low potential for the preservation of deeply buried bones (Surabian 2012).

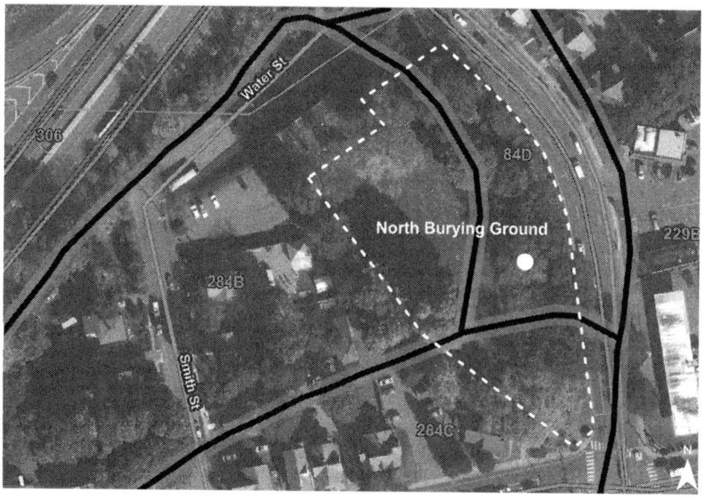

Fig. 5.2: A Web Soil Survey map showing the approximate boundary of the North Burying Ground and the location of the unrecorded burial vault (white dot).

A brief reconnaissance GPR survey was completed at this site using the SIR-4000 data acquisition system with a 400 MHz antenna. Several GPR traverses were conducted across the grass covered, sloping area located immediately upslope from the exposed vault door. These traverses were conducted to provide an estimate of the size and dimensions of this buried structure. The collected radar profiles were submitted to standard processing procedures of time-zero correction and background removal, with suitable color table and transform selections. The average velocity of pulse propagation and the depth scale were estimated by hyperbola matching.

Figure 5.3 contains two radar profiles that were collected over the expected location of the buried structure. The profile on the left (Fig. 5.3, A) was collected in an east–west direction that was conducted parallel with and 1 m behind the unearthed doorway; the profile on the right (Fig. 5.3, B) began 1 m behind the door and was conducted moving away from the unearthed feature in an upslope direction.

In the upper 20 cm of each radar profile, point and segmented linear reflections patterns are evident. As soil horizons (Ap and Bw) within the solum of Paxton and Montauk soils are weakly expressed and typically not distinguishable with GPR, these patterns were interpreted as layers of soil disturbance and added borrow materials. On both radar profiles, the inserted white arrows indicate the top of the Cd horizon and the interface that separates the soil solum from the denser substratum.

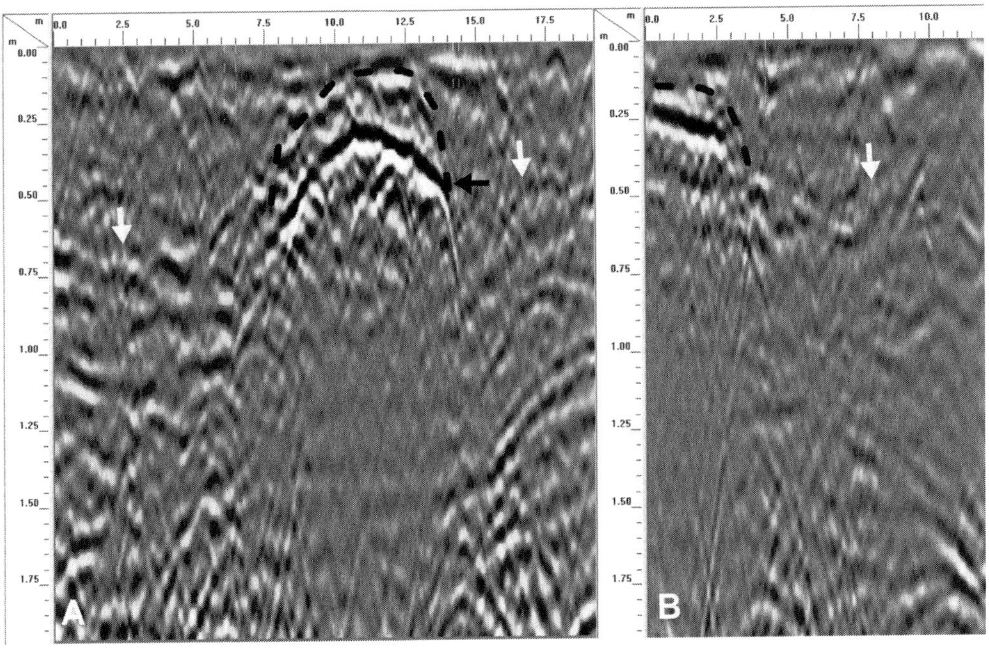

Fig. 5.3: Radar profiles from two traverses that were conducted upslope, and either parallel (left) or orthogonal (right) to the exposed vault's door. On each radar profile the interpreted outer edge of the vault's mortared brick wall has been highlighted by a dashed, black line.

Examining the radar profile shown in Figure 5.3, A, a distinct area of higher amplitude, curvilinear reflection patterns is noticeable between the 8.3–13.5 m distance marks and between depths of 11–55 cm. The dashed, black line has been used to highlight the interpreted top and outer edges to these reflection patterns and the buried structure. The highlighted structural features appear to have a very pronounced arched or rounded appearance suggesting that the structure has a rounded or gabled roof. However, a closer inspection and measurements reveal that this interface varies in depth by only about 45 cm over a lateral distance of about 5.2 m. The vertical exaggeration (about 12:1) of the radar profile, variations in slope contour and soil thickness, and the positioning of the antenna as it was moved along the traverse line can account for this inflated appearance.

In Figure 5.3, A, the highlighted area contains several closely spaced, contrasting reflection patterns that appear to be arranged in distinct bands. As these dissimilar reflection patterns are closely spaced, their reflections have been obliterated or obscured by constructive and destructive interference (Conyers 2013). As a consequence, their actual structure, thickness, and number are uncertain. The upper portion of the highlighted structure appears to consist of a mixed pattern of moderate to high amplitude, linear and point reflections. This varied reflection pattern suggests the possible presence of stones, weathered and fractured bricks, and mortar along this interface. Below this interface, a second, more noticeable and continuous reflection pattern is apparent that consists of high amplitude, curvilinear reflection bands. The polarity of these reflection bands appears to be reversed (Fig. 5.3, A, black arrow); changed from positive (white over black bands) to negative (black over white bands). A reversal in polarity indicates that the dielectric permittivity of the upper layer (the mortared brick wall) is higher than that of the lower layer (Leach 2021). Higher dielectric materials retain electromagnetic energy for longer periods of time and therefore prolong the time required for pulses of energy to travel through them (i.e., lowering the velocity of propagation). Based on this reasoning and with uncertainty attached, this interface is interpreted as representing the ceiling of the vault. The reversal of the polarity along this interface is assumed to be the result of an air-filled cavity (E_r = 1) underlying the stone and/or brick (E_r about 4) lined and mortared (E_r about 6) ceiling to the buried vault. Partially absorbed into the lower part of this continuous reflection pattern is a partially obscured interface that is composed of discrete point reflectors. The identity of this third interface could not be interpreted with any degree of confidence. It is also assumed that the contents of the vault and its floor are not visible due to the large scattering loses and pulse attenuation at the ceiling's stone/air interface, which has reflected most of the available radar energy and created a 'data shadow' below (Leach 2021). A 'data shadow' represents an area of low amplitude or no reflections on radar profiles.

Figure 5.3, B shows a radar profile from a traverse that was conducted in an upslope direction and away from the unearthed vault door. This traverse was started about 1 m behind the front of the structure (Fig. 5.3, B, top left corner) due to a pile of obstructing debris (see Fig. 5.1, A), and ran at a right-angle away from the exposed entrance. Conspicuous, linear patterns of high amplitude reflections are evident between depths of 16 cm and 28 cm in the upper left corner of this profile. A dashed, black line has been used to outline the interpreted top and outer edges to these reflection patterns and the buried structure. Like the radar profile shown in Figure 5.3, A, these varied reflection patterns can be subdivided into an upper layer composed of point and layered reflections, a middle segment consisting of high amplitude layered reflection bands, and a lower layer composed of point reflections. Collectively, the sloping pattern of these interfaces extend 2.5 m along the radar profile and are assumed to represent the structure of the buried vault. Adding that this traverse began 1 m away from the vault's entrance, the structure appears to extend about 3.5 m into the slope. As the traverse was orientated directly upslope from the vault's entrance, the apparent 18 cm dip in this reflection pattern is attributed to the added borrowed materials and thickening soil column.

Additional radar traverses were conducted over this site to help confirm the dimensions and shape of the buried structure. Based on an assessment of all radar profiles collected at this site, the approximate dimensions (5.2 × 3.5 m), depth to (11–55 cm), and shape (rectangular) of the tomb were revealed with GPR. While the reflection pattern that represents the outer surface and interior ceiling to this structure has been identified, uncertainties exist over the interpretation of the underlying reflection patterns and the identification of the vault's cavity and floor.

The GPR images of the ceiling of the vault and the cavity of the tomb gave us the dimensions of the structure, including depth. However, the Danbury Historical Society wanted to know if any burials were still in the tomb.

The tomb door was mortared closed, the iron hinges rusted and, not wanting to damage the structure in order to inspect the interior, we enlisted Dr Ronald Beckett, professor emeritus from Quinnipiac University's Bioarchaeological Laboratory, Department of Diagnostic Imaging, to conduct an endoscopic inspection. The endoscope employed consisted of a small lens connected by a flexible fiber optic cable that was attached to a handheld monitor. This technology was originally designed to examine the interior of human mummies. Using a hammer drill, Ron created a 1 inch (2.5 cm) diameter hole through the top middle of the tomb, inserted the endoscope, and took five photographic images of the interior.

The images were furnished to Collin Harty, exhibit designer at the Connecticut State Museum of Natural History, University of Connecticut. Collin uploaded the endoscopic images into a graphic design software program that assembled Ron's photos together into a single composite image of the tomb's interior (Fig. 5.4). The image clearly shows a pile of desiccated coffin wood toward the back end of the tomb, however there are no visible skeletal remains present. The coffins appeared to have been originally stacked along the back and sidewalls of the tomb. Over time, the desiccation of the wood and the weight from stacking collapsed the coffins, fragmenting and sprawling them onto the tomb floor. No brass tacks or nameplates were visible on any of the coffin lids. Brass

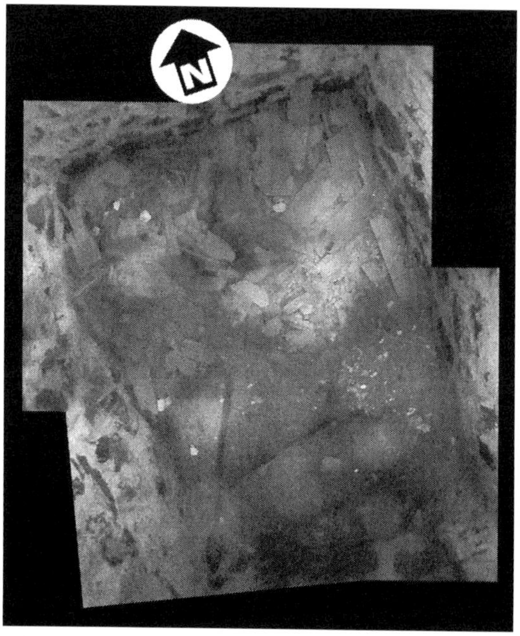

Fig. 5.4: Endoscopy image of the interior of the Dr Jabez Starr family tomb. Note the pile of wood along the rear (north) and sidewalls, and the absence of wood fragments near the front entrance of the tomb (lower right).

Fig. 5.5: The 'Starr & Clark' family mausoleum in the Wooster Cemetery, Danbury (Credit: Robert Young).

tacks were often hammered into the lid of the coffin, patterning the initials and age of death of the deceased. So, unfortunately, no genealogical identifications could be made based on the mortuary hardware.

In the past, whenever we have seen the collapse of stacked wooden coffins in other historical tombs, we have also observed human skeletal remains exposed between the wooden planks and dispersed throughout the floor of tombs. However, no human remains were exposed in any of the Starr Tomb interior images, which suggests that the bodies might have been removed at some point in the past, most likely to another cemetery. It appears that the wooden coffins had already broken apart and the human remains had skeletonized by the time of their removal.

Dr Jabes Starr appears to have built the North Burying Ground tomb about 1804, which coincided with the death of a daughter who died in infancy, but the mystery as to why we found the tomb empty remained. That is, until subsequent research by Bob Young, located an above-ground 'Starr' mausoleum in Wooster Cemetery across town. Wooster Cemetery's first burial dates to 1736, however, the modern cemetery was dedicated by the Danbury Cemetery Association in 1850. Based on existing 19th century records, the Starr family's Wooster Cemetery plot was purchased by Eliza A. Clark on 1 March 1882. Eliza, Jabes Starr's granddaughter, appears to have built the new mausoleum and arranged for the remains of her grandfather and her previously deceased family members to be removed from the North Burying Ground tomb and re-interred in the new mausoleum. Hence, the older tomb was sealed and covered with earth to obscure its earlier existence. Skeletal remains may have been placed in contemporary coffins and transferred to Wooster Cemetery in the mid-1880s. The panel sealing the front door of the new tomb reads *Families of Doctor Jabes Starr and James Clark - A.D. 1804 & 1877.*

Part II

Historical places and events

Chapter 6

Barkhamsted Lighthouse Village, Barkhamsted

Around 1740, a British American woman named Mary (Molly) Barber married a Narragansett Indian named James Chaugham. Molly's father disapproved of the marriage, and as a consequence, Molly and James Chaugham left her Connecticut Valley home and fled into the remote and unpopulated area of north-western Connecticut. Here, they settled and built their home on a terrace to the West Branch of the Farmington River at the base of Ragged Mountain (*Connecticut History* nd).

James and Mary Chaugham would raise eight children who would form the nucleus of a small, poor, ethnically diverse community composed of people of Native American, African, and European descent (Feder 1994). The Chaugham descendants remained in the village until it was abandoned in 1860. During this period, the trail along the base of Ragged Mountain was improved for stagecoach traffic. According to legend, in the early 19th century, the small community gained the title of the 'Lighthouse' settlement. Stagecoaches traveling on the Farmington River Turnpike saw either the lights or smoke coming from the home fires in this small community as a 'beacon' indicating that they were only a few miles away from their next stop in the nearby town of New Hartford (*Today in Connecticut History* 2019).

Today, the Barkhamsted Lighthouse Village is located within the Peoples State Forest, which was established in 1924 by the Connecticut Forest and Park Association with support from such groups as the Daughters of the American Revolution and the Connecticut Federation of Women's Clubs. The Village site was listed on the National Register of Historic Places in 1991 as Lighthouse Archeological Site (5-37). In 2008 the Connecticut Historic Preservation Council designated the Lighthouse Archaeological Site as a State Archaeological Preserve.

The site of the Lighthouse community is today covered by a thick forest canopy. Archaeological investigations were conducted at this site by Dr Kenneth Feder and students from Central Connecticut State University in 1986, 1990, 1991, and 2009. Preliminary 'walkover' or pedestrian surveys of the site revealed remnants of ten structures (six with stone foundations), four charcoal kilns, five stone quarries, a stone mortar, a well, and a cemetery (Feder 2009). Dr Feder's students have excavated 30, one-meter-square units, and 15, two-meter-square units across the Barkhamsted Lighthouse Village site (Feder 1994). These excavations have produced over 12,500 artifacts.

Located within the Archaeological Preserve is the Lighthouse Village Cemetery (41.94265 N. lat., 73.0066 W long.). This cemetery is believed to contain the graves of 50 to as many as 200 people who lived in the Lighthouse community, including the village's founding couple, Mary and James Chaugham. However, the gravestones that are evident consist of simple field stones that lack inscriptions (Fig. 6.1) and some gravesites could be unmarked. There are no intentions to disturb this cemetery by archaeological excavations.

Across the cemetery, the unmarked and upright fieldstones are believed to represent gravestones. Some of these fieldstones could be either headstones or footstones, while others could have been simply moved and placed upright by workers during the construction of a bordering stockade wall. This wooden stockade wall was erected around the cemetery during the 1930s by the Civilian Conservation Corps (CCC: Fig. 6.2). While the stockade wall has disintegrated and vanished, subtle linear surface features are believed to mark where it once stood. A carefully visual examination of the cemetery has revealed indistinct, linear trenches surrounding what is assumed to be the cemetery boundary. While the area enclosed by these trenches contains the bulk of the unmarked, upright fieldstones, pedestrian surveys conducted by archaeologists have recognized additional fieldstones outside its limits (Fig. 6.3). At the request of the Barkhamsted Historical Society, a GPR survey was conducted to ascertain the suitability of this geophysical method for detecting graves and to confirm the location of the former CCC stockade fence at the Barkhamsted Lighthouse Village Cemetery.

A Web Soil Survey map of the area surrounding the Lighthouse Village Cemetery is shown in Figure 6.4. The white square identifies the approximate location of the cemetery on this image. The Lighthouse Village Cemetery is located within a soil delineation that is labeled '73C', which indicates an area of Charlton-Chatfield complex on 0–15% slopes,

Fig. 6.1: The Barkhamsted Lighthouse Village Cemetery, facing west towards the West Branch of the Farmington River. Gravestones are unadorned field stones.

Fig. 6.2: Historical photograph of the wooden stockade wall that was erected in the 1930s by the Civilian Conservation Corps. (Credit: Mills 1952)

which is very stony. The well drained, very deep (>150 cm to bedrock) Charlton and moderately deep (50–100 cm to bedrock) Chatfield soils formed in loamy melt-out till over either schist, granite, or gneiss bedrock. Stones (rock fragments >35 cm in diameter) occupy 10– 25% of the exposed surface area and rock fragments (gravel, cobbles, stones, and boulders) compose 5–35% of the substratum. Depth to water table is greater than 203 cm (80 in). Both soils have very strongly acid reactions and therefore have low potential for the preservation of bones, wooden caskets, and other perishable features, which will decompose rapidly in these highly acidic soils (Surabian 2012).

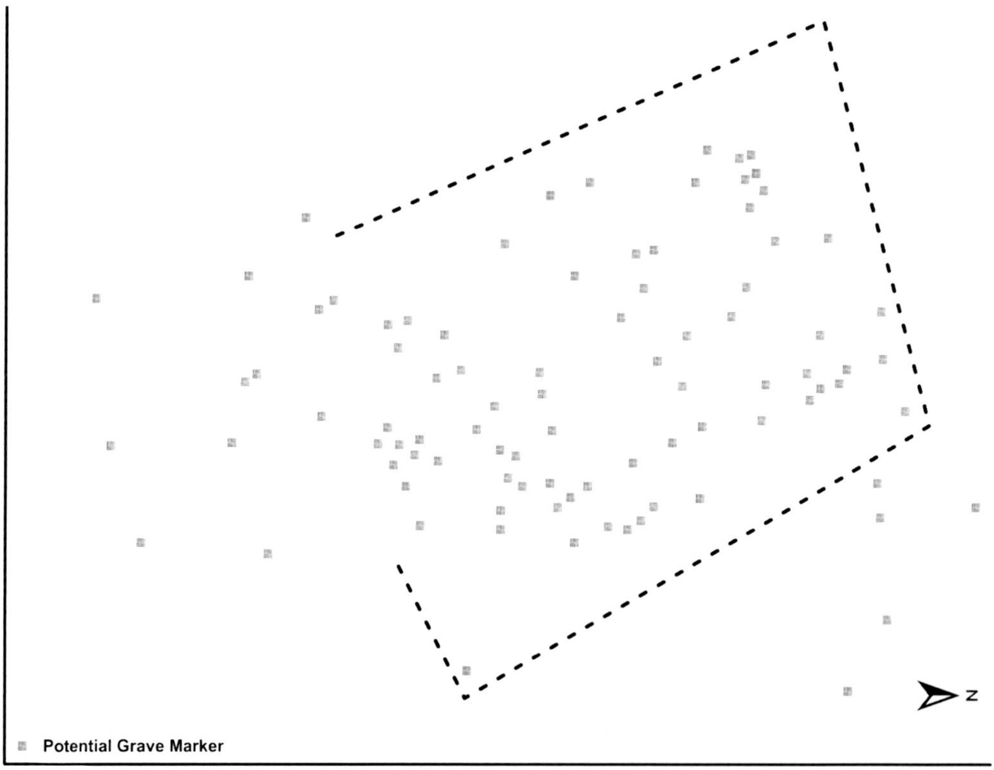

Fig. 6.3: A plan of the Lighthouse Village Cemetery showing the perceived location of the stockade wall (dashed line) and positions of fieldstones that could commemorate grave sites.

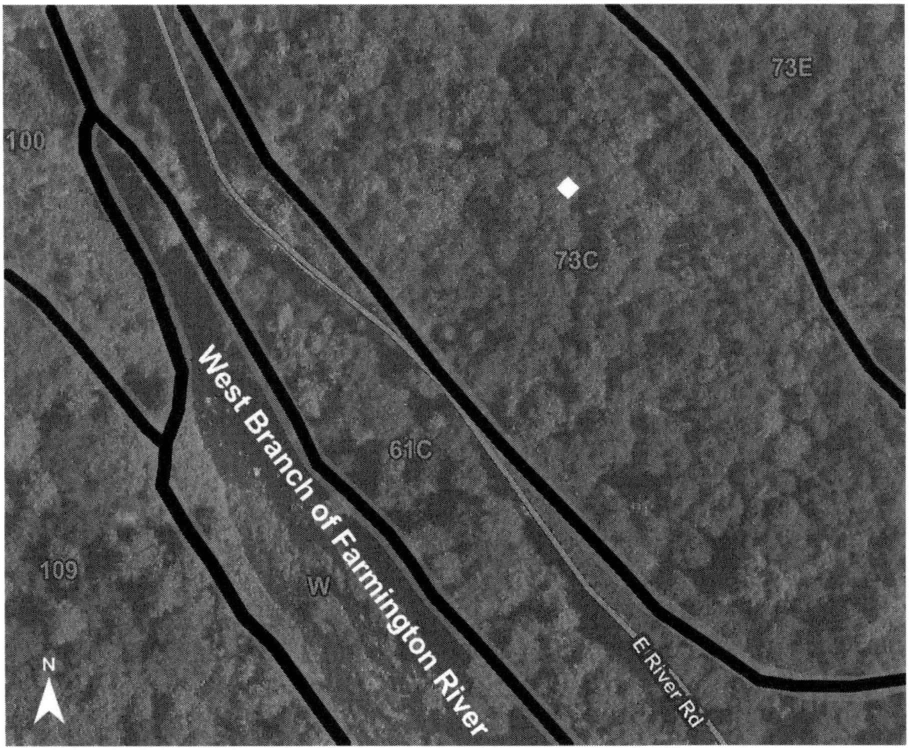

Fig. 6.4: A Web Soil Survey map of the area surrounding the former Lighthouse Village in Barkhamsted. The white square indicates the approximate location of the Lighthouse Village Cemetery.

Because of their low clay, moisture, and soluble salt contents Charlton and Chatfield soils are considered well suited to deep, high-resolution profiling with GPR. Nevertheless, the interpretation of graves with GPR was considered difficult due to the passage of time, the presence of a considerable number of rock fragments and tree roots, and the absence of highly contrasting soil or stratigraphic features. In addition, the substantial number of scattered fieldstones, trees, and gravestones on the surface of this site complicated radar survey design and execution.

Line or random walk GPR traverses were completed at the cemetery using the SIR-4000 data acquisition system with a 400 MHz antenna; both attached to a survey cart that was equipped with an odometer wheel. The collected radar profiles were submitted to standard processing procedures of time-zero correction and background removal, with suitable color table and transform selections. The average velocity of pulse propagation and the depth scale were estimated by hyperbola matching.

Figure 6.5 contains two, 2D radar profiles from the Lighthouse Village Cemetery. The radar profile shown in Figure 6.5, A was collected across an accessible area of Charlton soils. The considerable number of hyperbolic reflections evident in the upper 70 cm of this profile are believed to represent larger roots from nearby trees and scattered rock fragments. Other than the surface pulse there are no apparent reflections from soil horizons. The solum is not distinguishable from the substratum,

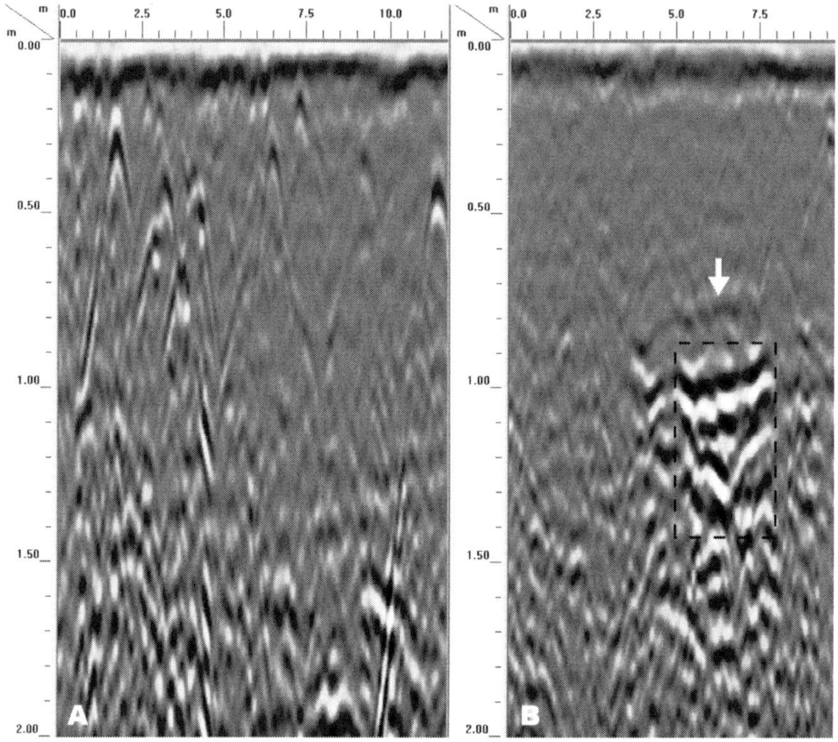

Fig. 6.5: The radar profile on the left (A) was collected within a relatively open area of the Lighthouse Village Cemetery. The profile on the right (B) was collected near several upright fieldstones that are believed to represent gravestones.

other than an increase in the number of reflections below a depth of about 1 m. There is no obvious reflection pattern on this radar profile to suggest either a burial or grave shaft.

A high amplitude, anomalous subsurface feature is evident on the radar profile shown in Figure 6.5, B. This profile was collected near upright fieldstones believed to represent gravestones. This feature is about 90 cm in depth and about 290 cm wide (enclosed by segmented black lines). The high amplitude, anomalous reflection pattern appears to consist of two sectors: an upper, slightly inclined, linear pattern and a lower chevron pattern. It is unclear whether the shallower reflection pattern represents one linear feature or four separate, but closely-spaced, point anomalies The deeper chevron-shaped reflection pattern appears more continuous. In addition, the polarity of these two patterns appears to be reversed; changed from positive (white over black bands) to negative (black over white bands). However, the two reflection patterns are too closely spaced to confirm this interpretation. A reversal in polarity would indicate that the dielectric permittivity of the upper layer is higher than that of the lower layer (Leach 2021). If a reversal in pulse polarity actually occurs, it could suggest the possibility of an air-filled void and a buried crypt. However, as the

Lighthouse Village community was poor and impoverished, it is questionable whether a long-lasting structure such as a brick-lined crypt could have been afforded. Another noteworthy feature on this radar profile is the weaker reflection pattern (identified by the white arrow) that overlies the aforementioned feature(s). This could represent a layer of mixed or dissimilar materials used to refill an excavation.

Figure 6.6 is a radar profile from a traverse that followed the center line of a linear trench on the south side of the cemetery. While conducting this radar traverse, the trench was noticeable for the first 6–7 m (span indicated by black segment line in Fig. 6.6) of this profile, after which it became more difficult to discern as it tapered into the adjoining, undisturbed surface area. It was observed that the trench contained a thicker mantle of accumulated leaves and moderately to highly decomposed organic materials than the surrounding, more level ground surface. This organic mantle would produce a less abrupt and contrasting air/soil contact than areas adjacent to the trench where the mineral soil was at or nearer to the surface. Within the obvious trench, the surface pulse consists of low amplitude reflections that indicate a less abrupt and contrasting interface. This radar traverse was continued out of the observed trench from the 7.5–11 m distance marks. Here, the surface pulse is of higher amplitudes suggesting a more abrupt and contrasting air/soil interface.

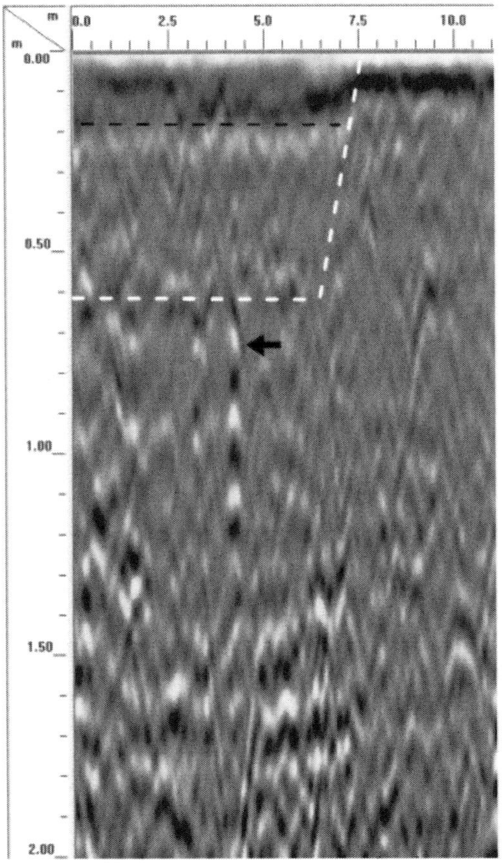

Fig. 6.6: A radar profile taken over the shallow, linear trench along the south side of the Lighthouse Village Cemetery. The black dashed line indicates the visible extent of a shallow trench. The white dashed line indicates the extent of the area that was interpreted as once occupied by the former stockade wall.

Two white segment lines have been inserted on Figure 6.6 to identify the interpreted location of the former stockade wall. The deeper, white, horizontal, segmented line represents the interpreted excavated depth of the wall. An irregular, but horizontal pattern of moderate–high amplitude reflections are apparent along this line. These are associated with soil compaction and higher bulk densities along the former base of the wall. The black arrow on this radar profile identifies a reverberating reflection pattern associated with a discarded metallic object which could have been deposited during the construction of the former wall.

The radar profiles from this brief GPR survey have helped to substantiated thoughts as to the location of south-west corner a former wooden stockade wall and aroused other thoughts concerning the presence, conditions, and nature of burials within the Lighthouse Village Cemetery. A large subsurface anomalous feature(s) was detected having unexpected and 'grave-like' characteristics. Interpretations of the different reflection patterns were biased by their presence within the subsurface of a cemetery. While results are interpretive, they provide additional information into the history and nature of this site.

Chapter 7

The 1814 Battle of Essex's Riverfront, Essex

Essex Village is on a peninsula that extends outwards from the western shore of the Connecticut River about 9.7 km (6 miles) upstream from its mouth on Long Island Sound. From 1648 to 1820, Essex Village was known as Pettipaug (Roberts 2020). During the 18th and 19th centuries, the three coves (North, Middle, and South) that were protected by the Pettipaug Peninsula provided shelter for the construction of wooden sailing ships (Fig. 7.1). The short distance from Long Island Sound made Pettipaug not only a significant ship-building center but a major trade center as well. In the late 1700s, ships from Pettipaug traded with the other colonies and the West Indies.

During the War of 1812, the United States embargo and the British blockade of the eastern end of Long Island Sound had severely impacted Pettipaug's trade and the shipbuilding industry. As a consequence, ship builders in Pettipaug refitted merchant ships into privateers. These armed vessels were authorized to capture British merchant ships and to bring their captured plunder back to port for resale.

The British knew of the shipyards and the privateers that were being built in Pettipaug (Roberts 2020). On the night of 7 April 1814, a British raiding party consisting of 136 Royal Marines and sailors under the command of Captain Richard Coote rowed boats from HMS *Borer*, *Endymion*, *La Hogue*, and *Maidstone* up the Connecticut River under the cover of darkness to burn the American ships at Pettipaug. After rowing pass an undefended fort on Saybrook Point near the mouth of the Connecticut River, the British landed early on the morning of 8 April along the waterfront at the foot of Pettipaug's Main Street (Fig. 7.1) and proceeded to torch 25 vessels tied along the wharves, on building stocks in shipyards, and at anchor in the three coves and along the Connecticut River (Fig. 7.2). The British did not burn the village of Pettipaug. By 10 am, the British completed their mission at Pettipaug and departed, sailing downriver in two captured 'prize ships', the *Young Anaconda* and the *Eagle*. Experiencing difficulties in keeping steerage against adverse winds, the *Young*

Fig. 7.1: A depiction of Pettipaug, Connecticut, in 1814 created by Robert VanKeirsbilck (Credit: Connecticut River Museum, Essex, CT).

Fig. 7.2: Painting exhibited at the Connecticut River Museum depicting British sailors and marines coming ashore at the Pettipaug waterfront and the burning of ships in the early morning of 8 April 1814 (Credit: Connecticut River Museum, Essex, CT).

Anaconda became grounded off Watrous Point, which is located only about 2 km (1.25 miles) south of Pettipaug Point (Roberts 2020). About 7 pm, Captain Coote decided to burn both ships and run the gauntlet of American rife and cannon fire along the Connecticut River under the cover of darkness in their ships' boats (Roberts 2020). The British returned to their ships on Long Island Sound after suffering the loss of two men. For the United States, the loss of 27 ships was the greatest single loss of American shipping during the entire war, and the largest loss of ships by the US until Pearl Harbor. Roberts (2020) noted that, at the time of the raid, the monetary loss to Pettipaug 'ranged between $150,000 and $200,000'. Unfortunately, as observed by Roberts, the British raid on Pettipaug would become 'the forgotten battle of the forgotten war'.

The British raiding party landed along the waterfront at the foot of Main Street in Pettipaug. This waterfront area has significant archaeological information and artifacts associated with the raid and the early history of the village. The first wharf was built here in 1656 near the Steamboat Dock building, the present home of the Connecticut River Museum. A former wharf is known to be buried under the museum's parking lot. The lot and museum are built on fill materials that were laid down in the 1840s when the waterfront was moved into deeper waters to accommodate the larger drafts of steamboats. In 1878, the Steamboat Dock building was built as a warehouse

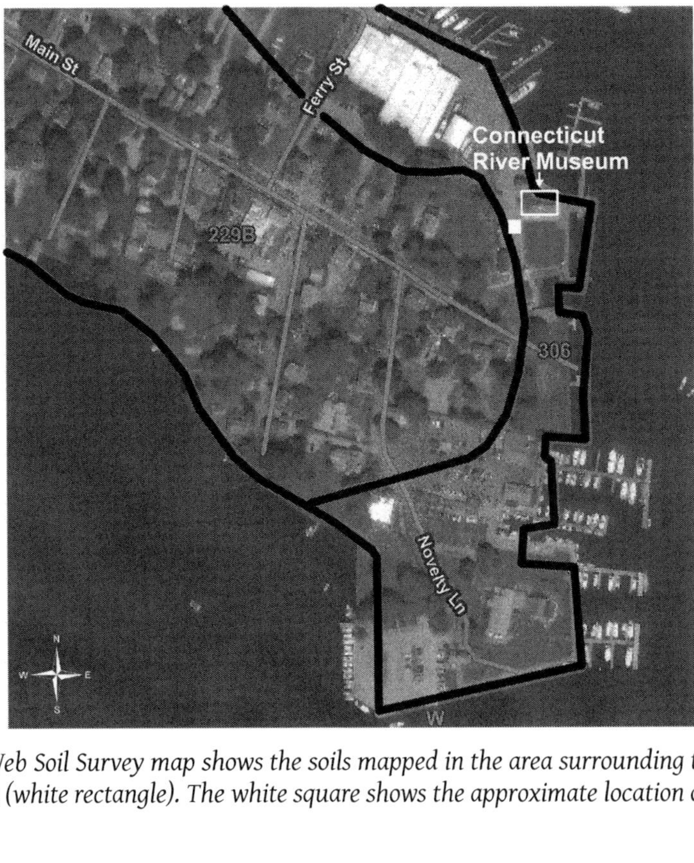

Fig. 7.3: This Web Soil Survey map shows the soils mapped in the area surrounding the Connecticut River Museum (white rectangle). The white square shows the approximate location of the GPR Grid.

and general store. In 1974, after falling into disrepair, the building was saved and converted into the Connecticut River Museum. This building is listed on Connecticut's State Register of Historic Places.

Historical maps and exploratory archaeological excavations have revealed the location of part of the town's original waterfront. The bulkheads along this waterfront provided mooring for ships and protected the shoreline from erosion. Archaeological excavations that were conducted in the late 1980s near the Connecticut River Museum revealed portions of the buried waterfront bulkhead, which historic records indicate was *c.* 90–120 m (300–400 ft) long. This buried bulkhead defines the approximate location of the town's waterfront during the War of 1812. The Connecticut River Museum is collecting information on this and other waterfront features in an effort to have the 'Essex Battle Sites' placed on the National Register of Historic Places and recognized by the National Park Service. To help further define the location of the buried wharf and other features of historic interest, the use of ground-penetrating radar (GPR) was proposed to the Connecticut State Archaeologist.

Based on findings from the 1989 archaeological excavations, an 11 × 11 m grid was established across a portion of the paved parking area located near the Connecticut River Museum, over a soil delineation that is labeled '306', denoting an area of Udorthents-Urban land complex (Fig. 7.3). Udorthents represents mineral soils that have been mapped at a more generalized level of classification. Udorthents have little or no evidence of soil development and lack sufficient information in USDA databases to provide a more specific classification or interpretations. In Connecticut, Udorthents are generally considered to be very deep (>1.5 m to bedrock), well drained soils developed mostly in glacial drift which has been altered or formed by humans. In urban areas, Udorthents identify soils that are either humanly transported material (HTM: e.g., fill) or humanly altered (e.g., truncated or mixed *in situ*) to a significant depth. Urban land is defined as land that is covered by pavement, buildings, and other impervious, manufactured surfaces and structures. Underlying these impermeable layers and structures, artificially altered or transported earthen materials, natural soil materials, or a mix of both can occur. Both Udorthents and Urban land can exhibit a wide range of physical and chemical properties that impact the effectiveness of GPR. In Connecticut, Udorthents are generally considered to have high potential and Urban land is not rated for the preservation of perishable objects (Surabian 2012).

The GPR survey was completed using the SIR-3000 data acquisition system with a 400 MHz antenna. Neither a GPR survey cart nor survey wheel was available for this survey. As a consequence, the setup on the SIR-3000 data acquisition system was changed from a distance-based to a time-based mode of operation. Time-based radar data contain no distance identifiers. In the time-based mode, the radar operator must attempt to move the antenna at a steady speed and insert user marks at measured intervals along each radar traverse line. During the post-processing, the time-based radar data were submitted to a distance normalization procedure. Distance normalization establishes a constant horizontal scale between the inserted user marks.

Fig. 7.4: Conducting the GPR grid survey across the parking area near the Connecticut River Museum. The 400 MHz antenna is being moved along a rope line that is marked at 1 m intervals.

Two parallel lines were laid out on the eastern and western sides of the proposed grid site (see white square on Fig. 7.3). Survey flags were inserted in the ground at 50 cm intervals along these boundary lines. A total of 23, 11 m long radar traverses were completed with the GPR system in a back and fore manner across the grid. Each traverse was conducted along a west-to-east trending grid line that was created by stretching a rope between matching flags on the two opposing boundary lines (Fig. 7.4). For distance control, the rope line that was marked at 1 m intervals. The collected radar profiles were submitted to time-zero correction, background removal, and distance normalization processing procedures, with suitable color table and transform selections. The average velocity of pulse propagation and the depth scale were estimated by hyperbola matching.

Figure 7.5 is a radar profile that was collected across the middle of the grid site. The profile contains two prominent column-like features. These are highlighted by rectangles formed of black, dashed lines. Similar column-like features appeared on a majority of the radar profiles that were collected across the grid site, though at different positions along the traverse lines. The crowns of these column-like features have high amplitude, relatively flat reflection patterns, which are bounded by shallower, inwardly sloping linear patterns. The 'pan-like' appearance of these reflection patterns suggests the settling over time of materials used to refill excavated pits or trenches. The soil materials that underlie these crowns display low amplitude reflections, a property that typically suggests non-contrasting and homogenous materials. However, the grid site adjoins a segment of the Connecticut River that is tidally influenced. Salt and brackish waters have high electrical conductivities which will rapidly attenuate radar signals. Soils and earthen materials affected by these waters are considered unsuited to GPR. It is possible that the intrusion of brackish waters from the Connecticut River into deeper soil layers and their subsequent mixing in the materials used to refill excavated trenchs or pits produced these columns of low signal returns. An alternative interpretation is that the contrasting materials in the crowns of these column-like features are more highly conductive and have severely attenuated the radar signal producing an underlying data shadow (Leach 2021).

Three additional features have been labelled on the radar profile in Figure 7.5. The high amplitude, linear reflection pattern labeled 'A' forms a prominent, horizontally layered feature across a majority of the deeper portion of this profile. The continuity of this linear reflection pattern appears to be disrupted and hidden by the previously mentioned column-like features. Two conspicuous high amplitude reflection patterns are identified near 'B'. As this is a historical site, it is possible that these reflection anomalies represent buried artifacts. Along the right-hand (eastern) boundary of this radar profile, a portion of a large hyperbola ('C') is evident. On a majority of the radar profiles collected across this site, similar and even higher amplitude hyperbolas occurred along either or both the eastern and wesern grid boundaries. However, like the other anomalies on radar profiles, GPR detects but does not identify the features.

Four depth-slice amplitude images from the grid site are shown in Figure 7.6. These depth-slices correspond to estimated soil depths of 0 cm, 50 cm, 100 cm, and 150 cm. For display purposes, each of the depth-slice amplitude images is viewed from directly overhead looking downwards into the grid.

The 0 cm depth-slice image contains a cluster of small, high amplitude (red) point reflections. Unfornuately, the features causing these anomalous reflection patterns were obscured from visual observations by the pavement. However, as they occur within or directly below the pavement, they were not considered of historical interest.

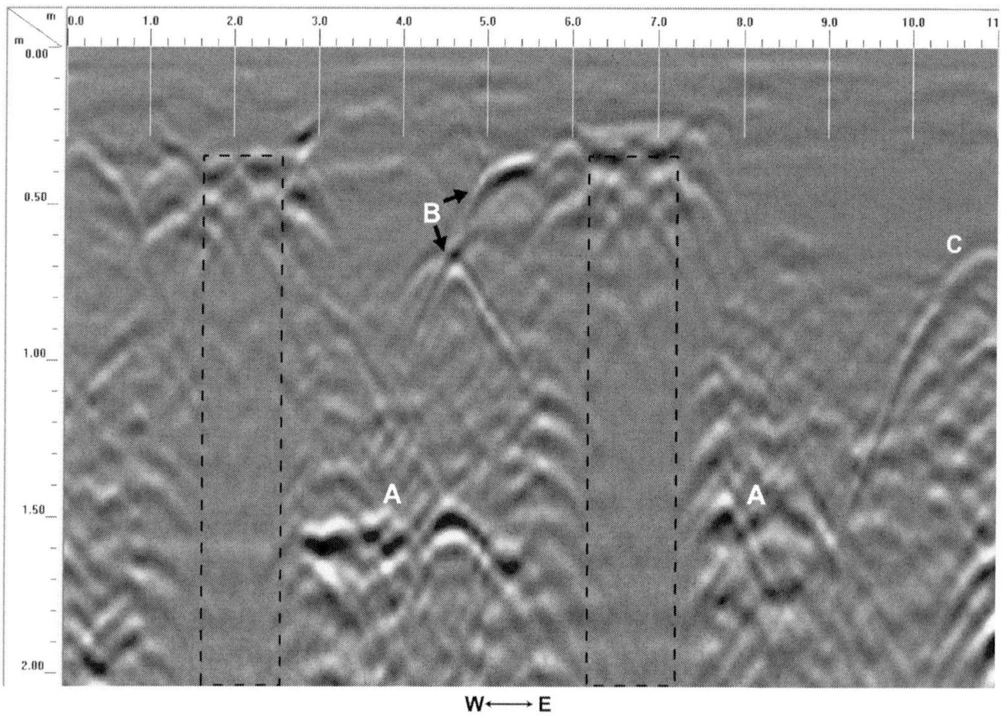

Fig. 7.5: A representative profile from the grid site at the Connecticut River Museum. This profile was taken along a west-east trending grid line.

With the exception of these patterns, the remainder of the 0 cm depth-slice images appears comparatively homogenous and nondescript, consisting principally of low amplitude reflections.

On the 50 cm depth-slice image, four moderate to high amplitude, rectangular-shaped patterns have been highlighted by black dashed lines. These patterns are narrow with their long axes extenting in an north–south direction beneath the grid site. These patterns appear to range from about 1.7 m to 2 m wide and 4.6–6.3 m long. The two lower rectangular-shaped patterns appear to be subdivided into two sections along their long axes. The sections appear to range from about 2 m to 3.8 m long. These anomalous patterns are believed to indicate the locations of former excavations or test-trenches that have been refilled with contrasting, mixed soil materials.

On the 100 cm and 150 cm depth-slice images, two high amplitude, linear reflection patterns are apparent along the northern portion of the western, and the southern portion of the eastern, borders of the grid site. These features are identified with black dashed lines. These reflection patterns could represent portions of former bulkheads. In addition, on the 150 cm depth-sliced image, the outline of a large rectangular-shaped feature has been highlighted by black dashed lines. This

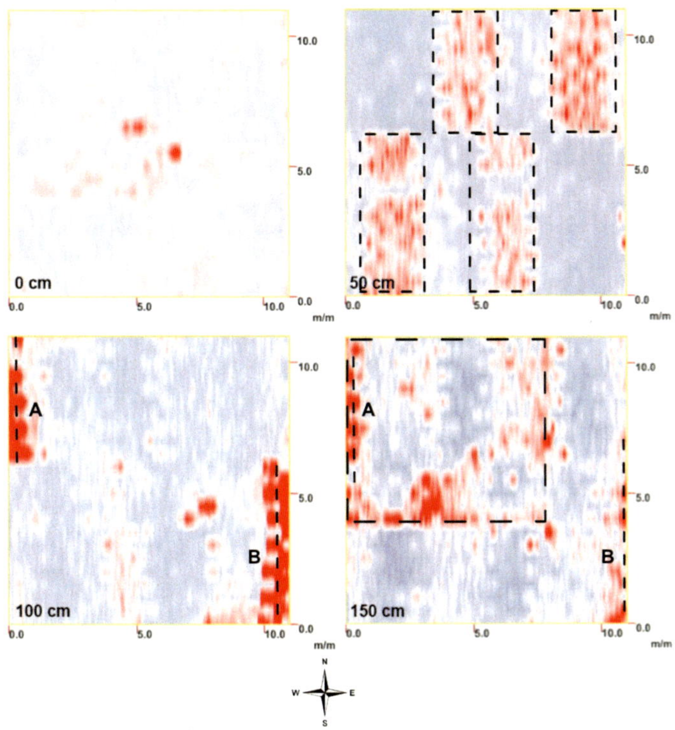

Fig. 7.6: Four depth-slice amplitude images of the grid site showing patterns that likely represent former human structures.

feature incorporates the linear reflection pattern that was previously identified along the western boundary of the grid. This large rectangular-shaped feature could represent the remnants of a bulkhead wharf which had been 'constructed by stacking and interlocking the ends of long timbers' (Greenburg 2006). Bulkhead wharves were constructed by erecting walls parallel with the shoreline, then filling in or fastening with back-braces to the land. On the 150 cm depth-slice image, high amplitude (red) linear reflection patterns are apparent within the area highlighted by black dashed lines. These anomalous features could represents remnants of the former wharf.

Ground-penetrating radar provided a fast, non-invasive and cost-effective method of recording and examining a buried historic waterfront of the early 19th century village of Pettipaug. The study site was located in an area of humanly transported materials covered by pavement. In Connecticut, although HTM have complex and often unpredictable spatial and vertical variability in their physical and chemical properties, they are considered to be generally well suited to deep, high-resolution GPR profiling. Radar profiles and depth-slice amplitude images from this site revealed anomalous subsurface features and distinct spatial patterns which were associated with refilled excavation pits or trenches, a buried historic bulkhead wharf, and suggestion of possible saltwater intrusion.

Chapter 8

A pandemic strikes: Old Farm Cemetery, Middletown

Overflow cots to care for the numerous sick were lined up along Middlesex Hospital corridors when regularly allotted beds and rooms were filled to capacity. Doctors and nurses were overwhelmed and understaffed, some even contracting the virus and dying of the infection along with their patients. Urgent calls were sent out for retired health care workers to assist and for any volunteers with medical training and experience to lend a hand. Sporting events, fairs, and theater performances were cancelled; schools were closed. People were encouraged to wear muslin masks, maintain distances from each other and quarantine. Nonetheless, in Middletown, Connecticut, deaths occurred so fast that corpses were placed in the streets since there was no longer enough space at local morgues or funeral parlors to accommodate all of the deceased. The pandemic seemed like a plague of Biblical proportions.

The preceding paragraph may sound like a modern news release describing the 2020 COVID-19 pandemic but, actually, the description was gleaned from newspaper accounts of the 1918 worldwide flu pandemic and how it afflicted the citizens of Middletown, Connecticut, where over 400 people died and an estimated total of 1400 were infected (Savas 2004, 2). Primary sources suggest that the community responded with a spirit of co-operative unity against an invisible common enemy to overcome fear and uncertainty. When corpses lined the streets and sidewalks of Middletown, local residents drove around town to load bodies into cars and wagons and cart them away (Savas 2004, 18–19). Masked work crews dug individual graves, hurriedly placing influenza victims into the ground. The labor had to be done expeditiously as contagion stalked the volunteers. There was no time for personal identifications, no time to construct coffins, no time for burial markers, no time for religious ceremonies (Fig. 8.1).

And, apparently, there was no time to log the interments officially into the city's death or cemetery records since city archives do not chronicle burial locations

(Middletown Death Records 1921). So, within three generations, no local cultural memory of where the victims of the 'Spanish Lady' were laid to rest could be found. However, almost 100 years after the horrific pandemic, Cemetery Superintendent and lifetime Middletown resident, August 'Augie' DeFrance, was told by an elderly town resident that a series of ground-level depressions in the rear portion of Old Farm Hill Cemetery were associated with city's pandemic fatalities. Based on his intuition and research, Augie called the Office of State Archaeology for assistance.

The 1918 influenza pandemic appeared to have been confined to the annals of history until COVID-19 pandemic struck. Soon thereafter, researchers of the contemporary pandemic were delving into historical records to understand better what transpired in 1918 as a precedent for the modern malady.

While there is no agreed upon theory as to where the 1918 virus originated in the US, one theory is that it occurred at Fort Riley, Kansas, where the first cases were recorded in early March 1918 (Crosby 2003). Four hundred and fourteen Fort Riley soldiers were infected; 48 died. This world-wide pandemic is known as the 'Spanish Flu' or 'Spanish Lady' because it was first widely reported in neutral Spain, where wartime censorship was not needed. World War I and the movement of soldiers throughout the world helped transmit the disease globally. Though the first wave was relatively mild, mutated strains would be unleashed, leading to an estimated 500 million infections (a third of the world's population at that time) and 50–100 million deaths internationally (Barry 2004, 4). No-one was safe and, without effective antibiotics, no effective remedy was available.

Previous influenza deaths afflicted mainly the elderly and the infirmed most severely. However, what made the 1918 outbreak unique and so feared was that it infected persons between the ages of 20 and 40 the hardest; an age group usually at their strongest bodily phase to resist the virus; 8–10% of all young adults in the world died from the pandemic (Sava 2004, 8). Researchers believe that this particular virus stimulated a physiological reaction that released cytokine, a pro-inflammatory molecule that destroys the immune systems of the young (Barry 2004). Of Connecticut's 9000 documented deaths, 5000 were between 20 and 39 years of age (Acari and Birden 1997).

The death toll in Connecticut represented nearly 1% of the state's population in 1918 (Drury 2020). Most likely spreading from the New London seaport community, the virus moved north and westward into the state's interior (Arcari and Birden 1997). Especially hard hit were urban industrial and seaport communities, where population densities spread the influenza through crowded city neighborhoods, overwhelming poor immigrant communities. Many died in their homes, unable to get to hospitals, hence spreading the disease among family members and others sharing the same household.

Though every family was afflicted with the illness and everyone in the Middletown community lost kinfolk and friends, the city's immigrant community suffered and died disproportionately compared to other residents. The city's deaths were 14 times greater than the 2020 COVID-19 infection rates (Day 2020). Experiencing the recent pandemic, we deeply appreciate the heartbreak, the fear, and the devastation caused by the 1918 virus.

Old Farm Hill Cemetery is located in the southern portion of Middletown and dates back to the 1700s. The burying ground's entrance is along Ridge Road where the earliest tombstones reside on an elevated hilltop. The study area is situated in an open, grassy field that is tucked below the hilltop on the far backside of the cemetery adjacent to Ryan Street. There are no burial markers in this low-lying, hindmost section, but a series of subtle shallow, rectangular-shaped soil depressions are visible on the lawn. The cemetery superintendent, Augie DeFrance, wanted to know if these depressions might represent unmarked burials associated with hastily interred 1918 pandemic victims.

To greatly reduce exploration time and ground disturbances, a GPR investigation of the site was proposed. It was hoped that GPR could detect, without the need for digging, the existence of individual and/or mass graves and, if identified, provide a better understanding of the number and arrangement of these burials.

Prior to the GPR investigation, a soil map from the Web Soil Survey (Fig. 8.2) was reviewed to determine whether soil conditions at the Cemetery were suitable for GPR. The study site is located within a soil delineation labeled '33B'. This identifies an area of Hartford sandy loam on 3–8% slopes. The very deep (>1.5 m to bedrock), somewhat

Fig. 8.1: This photograph from the Middletown Press shows a flu patient during the flu pandemic of 1918 (Credit: Library of Congress, Prints & Photograph Division).

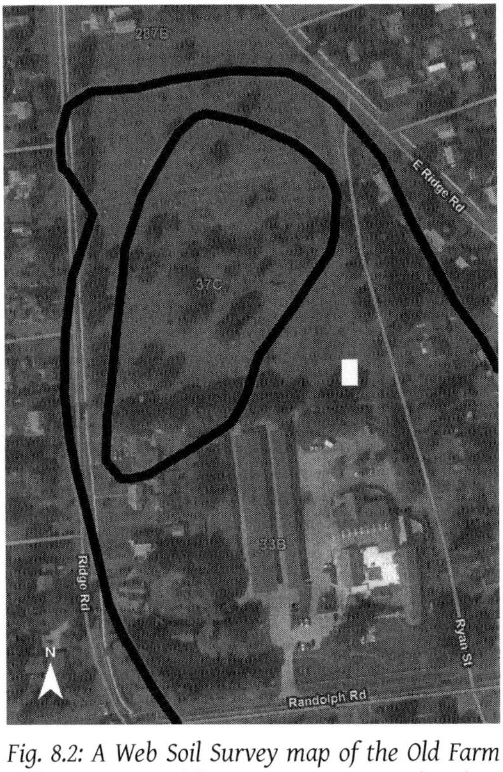

Fig. 8.2: A Web Soil Survey map of the Old Farm Hill Cemetery, Middletown, Connecticut. The white rectangle indicates the approximate location of the GPR grid.

excessively drained Hartford soils formed in sandy glacial outwash deposits. These soils primarily consist of stratified, reddish sands and gravels. Water is rapidly removed from these soils. As Hartford soils are sandy and very deep to a water table, they are easily excavated and therefore provide an ideal location for burials. Because they commonly lack free water and have low clay and soluble salt contents, they have relatively low electrical conductivities and are considered well suited to GPR. Hartford soils are considered to have medium potential for the preservation of bones and wooden caskets (Surabian 2012).

The survey was conducted with the SIR-4000 and a 400 MHz antenna; both attached to a survey cart that was equipped with an odometer wheel. The 400 MHz antenna provided suitable investigation depth and resolution of subsurface features in the profiled Hartford soils. The GPR data was collected within a small (11 × 22 m) grid that was established across a portion of the open lawn in the rear of the cemetery (white rectangle on Fig. 8.2; Fig. 8.3). Traverses were made with the GPR system along 23 parallel, north–south trending grid lines that were spaced 50 cm apart. These north–south sweeps by the GPR at intervals of 50 cm were considered adequate to capture the presence and extent of a traditional Christian burial. These burials would be positioned with the bodies extended in an east–west direction, at right-angles to the GPR traverses, thus ensuring their being passed over several times rather than missed (GPR traverses passing between burials).

Radar profiles collected along these traverse (grid) lines were submitted to standard processing procedures of time-zero correction and background removal, with suitable color table and transform selections. The average velocity of pulse propagation and the depth scale were estimated by hyperbola matching.

Fig. 8.3: A Google Maps photo of Old Farm Hill Cemetery showing the lawn where burials from the 1918 flu pandemic are believed to be located.

During data collection, a continuous real-time two-dimensional profile (radar profile) of the subsurface was viewed on the radar's control console. After one traverse, it was apparent that the soils were favorable for the use of GPR and the settings on the GPR console produced suitable data for interpretations. In general, the solum (A and Bw horizons) has a relatively uniform appearance with natural soil horizons that are too weakly expressed to be captured on radar profiles. The substratum (C horizons) is composed of stratified sands and gravels. These soil factors favor the detection of burials with GPR. Grave shafts excavated in these materials will cause the truncation of soil horizons and stratigraphic layers; refilled grave shafts will consist of mixed soil materials that contrast with the adjoining undisturbed soil structure and materials. However, one major concern was the large volume of rock fragments, which produced a high amount of 'clutter' that could obscure the recognition of some burials and the distinction of refilled grave shafts from the adjoining undisturbed outwash materials.

Figure 8.4 is a radar profile that was collected along a traverse line within the grid. An examination of the upper 25 cm of this profile reveals undulating bands of low amplitude (light red and blue) reflections with multiple breaks or discontinuities. The presence of these undulating, discontinuous bands suggests possible soil disturbances and the sequential addition of layers of fill materials. Starting at a depth of about 50 cm from the soil surface, the substratum appears as a chaotic pattern of high amplitude reflectors (bright red and blue). However, within this cluttered pattern, the overall reflection pattern suggests slightly tilted or sloping layers of contrasting outwash strata.

When human bodies, coffins, and grave goods are placed in the ground, the vertically excavated grave shaft is often distinguishable on GPR profiles. During excavation of a grave, the natural soil and substrate are typically placed on the surface nearby and then used to refill the grave shaft after interment. The excavated materials that are used to refill the grave shaft are highly mixed during this process, losing the former natural structure and the original horizontal layering of most naturally formed soils. In soils that have well expressed and strongly contrasting structures, the interpretation of grave shafts on GPR profiles, especially after the passage of many years, is possible.

Upon further inspection of the radar profile shown in Figure 8.4, there appear to be distinct, narrow vertical columns of contrasting reflection patterns that extend through both the solum (0–50 cm) and the substratum (>50 cm). These patterns are attributed to grave shafts that contain mixed backfilled materials which contrast with the surrounding natural soil and substrate. Six vertical columns of contrasting reflection patterns, each considered to represent a grave shaft, have been highlighted by dashed rectangles on the radar profile in Figure 8.4. Additional vertical patterns, though perhaps less distinct, can be identified on this radar profile. If these features are in fact grave shafts, they would attest to the occurrence of multiple, very-closely spaced graves.

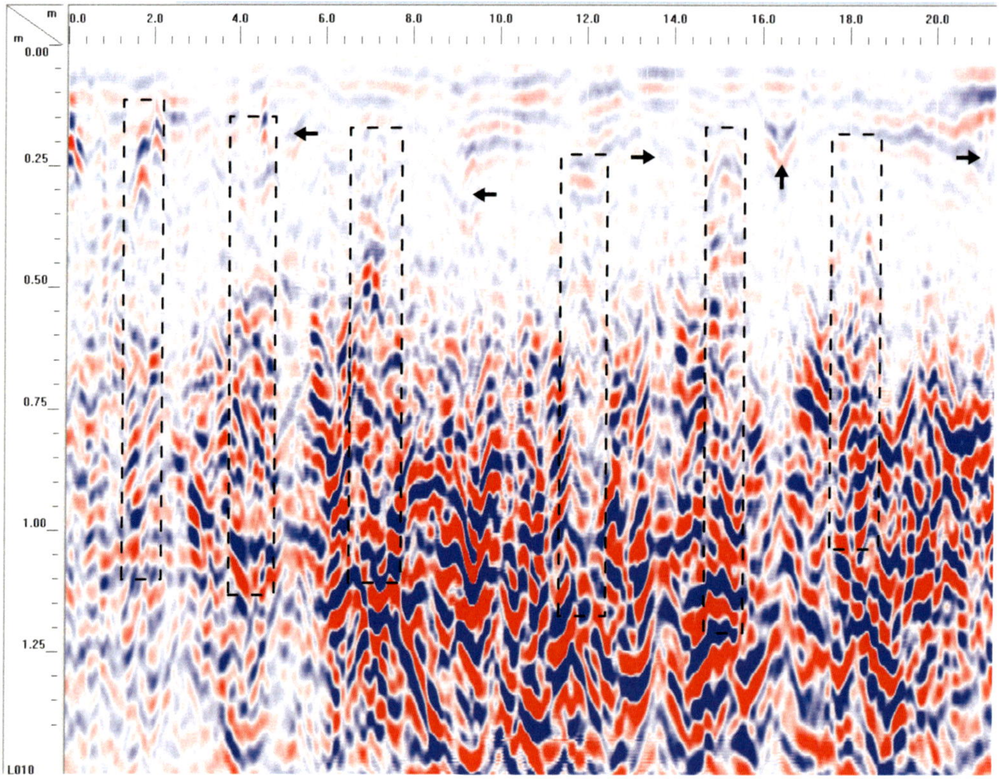

Fig. 8.4: A radar profile collected across the Old Farm Hill Cemetery GPR grid.

Reflection patterns at the bases of these suspected grave shafts are exceedingly varied and complex. Patterns supporting the presence of possible buried coffins or human remains are obscured by the large amounts of rock fragments present in the surrounding outwash deposits. The remnants of any cadaver or coffin, if present, do not stand out and are therefore difficult to identify with any degree of confidence. It is possible that a few of the suspected grave shafts may contain more than one closely spaced body and/or coffin. Stacked burials were not uncommon during this period.

With the passage of time, human remains decay and wooden coffins disintegrate causing the soil to settle over the refilled grave shaft. Black arrows have been used to identify several concave-upward reflection patterns that suggest possible soil slumping in the upper part of the radar profile shown in Figure 8.4. It was the observation of shallow, rectangular-shaped soil depressions by the cemetery superintendent that prompted this investigation.

Three depth-slice amplitude images from the grid site are shown in Figure 8.5. Depth-slice amplitude images are helpful in distinguishing and identifying potential targets and reducing interpretation uncertainties. These depth-slices correspond to estimated soil depths of 50 cm, 100 cm, and 150 cm. For display purposes, each depth-slice amplitude images is viewed from directly overhead looking downwards into the grid.

Looking at the three depth-slice images, there is a general increase in the number and amplitude of reflections with increasing soil depth. On the 50 cm depth-slice image, several moderate to high amplitude (red), linear reflection patterns are apparent. These patterns are narrow and appear to extent in an east-west direction across the grid site. High amplitude, contrasting, rectangular-shaped reflection anomalies that appear on depth-slice amplitude images are considered 'grave-like' and are often used to identify burials (Wadsworth *et al.* 2020). As these reflection patterns occur at relatively shallow soil depths, they could represent potential areas of soil disturbances and mixing. On the 100 cm and 150 cm depth-slice images, many high amplitude (bright red), roughly rectangular-shaped reflection patterns are evident. As these patterns are aligned and elongated in a general east to west orientation, they suggest probable graves. If necessary, one or more of these patterns could be excavated by a qualified archaeologist to confirm these interpretations.

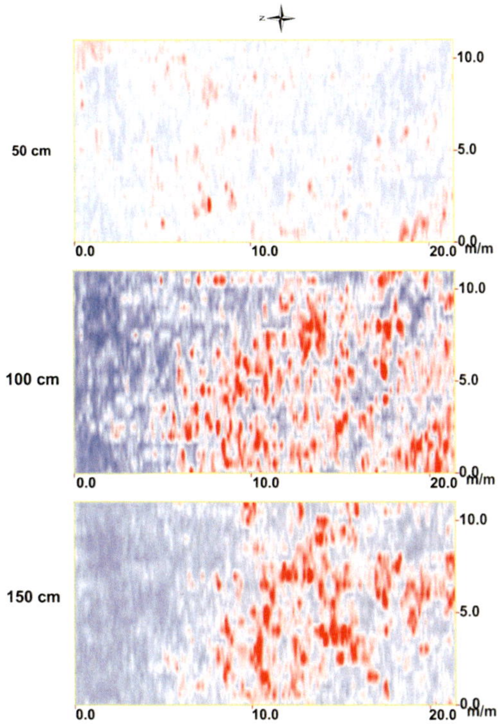

Fig. 8.5: Three depth-slice amplitude images of the grid site showing rectangular-shaped patterns that are elongated in an east-west direction and suggestive of graves.

Ground-penetrating radar was used to investigate the nature and reason for the rectangular shaped, slight depressions that were observed on the lawn at the backside of the Old Farm Hill Cemetery. Multiple, contrasting, columnar patterns were observed on radar profiles. These features were suspected to represent refilled grave shafts. Multiple 'grave-like' patterns, elongated in an east-west direction, were observed on depth-slice amplitude images. The reflection patterns that were evident on radar profiles and depth-slice images provide strong evidence supporting the likely presence and locations of unmarked burials in the Old Farm Hill Cemetery.

Chapter 9

Lt Eugene M. Bradley plane crash site, Windsor Locks

First Lieutenant Frank Mears, Commander of the 64th Pursuit Squadron, sauntered into the Ready Room where pilots were congregating for their daily training assignments. The Army Air Base in Windsor Locks, Connecticut, had opened only three days earlier on 18 August 1941, when the squadron had arrived. 'Who wants to go up for some one-on-one combat?' he inquired. Without hesitation, Second Lieutenant Eugene M. Bradley, who loved to fly, jumped from his seat and exclaimed excitedly, 'I'll go!'. 'Okay', Mears said, 'Get your gear!'

The two Army Air pilots were strapped into the cockpits of their Curtis P-40s and taxied to the runway. Bradley became airborne at 9:15 am with Mears following immediately behind him. They formed up at an altitude of 10,000 ft (*c.* 3000 m) then climbed to 15,000 ft (*c.* 4500 m) to conduct their 'Top Gun' style training exercises. Each man twisted and turned his aircraft in a descending corkscrew pattern trying to best the other. As they descended to about 5000 ft (*c.* 1500 m), Mears had Bradley in his sights and radioed for him to break off and start the exercise again. Both pilots veered hard to the left with Mears ascending. When Bradley did not appear, Mears dropped his left wing to locate him. Instead of climbing, Mears was horror-struck to see Bradley's plane in a slow downward spiral. He shouted into his radio for Bradley to pull out. There was no response, the plane continued to descend. Mears radioed again for Bradley to bail out, but there was no response to his second call. All Mears could do now was watch.

On the ground, military personnel and local tobacco farmers had been viewing the aerial maneuvers above them; now, they saw the nose-down spiral of the Curtis and heard the screeching of Bradley's engine. The P-40 stopped turning at 800 ft (*c.* 250 m) and quietly glided into the woods. No explosion; no fire; no sound; nothing, except the earth shaking beneath the spectators' feet.

Stunned, military and local people reacted. Private John Reese, an aircraft welder who had been working in the main hangar, ran out toward the crash site with other military personnel. Reese would hop onto a fire truck as it passed by him. Arriving at the crash site, Reese was assigned the task of digging by hand to recover the pilot.

Helen Kulas was working in the tobacco fields east of the airport when the crash occurred. Her brother, Frank, who was tending fields to the north, tried to reach the crash site but was stopped by Army personnel that had arrived beforehand. He would go back later.

The P-40 smashed into the ground nose first near the airport boundary. The engine rested at a depth of 3.9–4.6 m (13–15 ft) below the surface in a sparsely wooded area with sandy soil (Palshaw 2008). The only part of the plane visible above ground was its tail. Bradley was found still strapped into his seat. He had made no effort to bail out. The Army recovered the plane wreckage using heavy machinery and the subsequent crater was backfilled by a bulldozer. No record was ever made of the cause of the crash, though most believe that Bradley had blacked out during the hard left turn. If not tragic enough, Bradley's wife had travelled with him to Connecticut and was only 2 miles away in the village of Poquonock. She was five months pregnant when she felt the earth tremble not realizing it was from the impact of her husband's plane.

Although there are extensive military and medical records of what happened that day, none of these official documents notes the specific location of Bradley's crash site. Since the site was not documented, maybe due to security concerns with a possibly impending war, the knowledge of where Bradley crashed had been lost in public memory. Renewed interest in rediscovering the site arose with the publication of the history of Bradley Field in 1998 by the New England Air Museum (NEAM 1998). If documents were not helpful, the Museum wanted to know if archaeological and geophysical techniques could be used to locate the crash site. The Connecticut Office of State Archaeology was contacted in February 2005 for assistance, beginning five years of archival, oral histories and field research into locating the crash site. John Reese and the Kulas were among 14 eyewitnesses who were interviewed in 1998.

The Windsor Locks Army Air Field was situated on 1700 acres (*c.* 690 ha) of former tobacco farmland in Windsor Locks, Connecticut. The land had been purchased by the State of Connecticut and leased to the federal government for use as an Army Air Force Base in 1941. Lt Eugene M. Bradley's fatal accident is of historic significance, not only because it was the first crash to occur at this field, but because it led the War Department to rename the air field to the Army Air Base, Bradley Field (Palshaw 2018). After World War II, Bradley Field was deeded to the state of Connecticut and re-opened for public use in 1946. Today, Bradley Field is known as Bradley International Airport; Connecticut's busiest commercial airport and the second busiest airport in New England. Regrettably, the Airport has neither a picture of Lt Bradley nor an explanation of his legacy on display for public viewing.

Following the New England Air Museum's request for assistance, Connecticut Archaeological Center, University of Connecticut, and Friends of the Connecticut

State Archaeologist formulated a research design in an attempt to locate the crash site. With the assistance of the Connecticut Department of Transportation (CTDOT), the CT National Guard, Signature Flight Support, and Bombardier Aerospace, the research team gathered extensive information from state and military records, old aerial photographs of the airport (Fig. 9.1), newspaper articles, oral histories, and other sources concerning the crash. Twenty-one test criteria were developed to narrow the site search. Unfortunately, much has changed at Bradley International Airport making it difficult to pinpoint the crash site. While several potential sites had been identified, all archaeological testing yielded negative results. However, the most likely site was inaccessible, as it is located under Runway 15 of the International Airport (see Fig. 9.2). This runway was extended in the 1960s to allow jet airliners to land, and the suspected crash site was unknowingly paved over.

The aforementioned organizations approached Connecticut's Bureau of Aeronautics, which is a unit within the state's Department of Transportation, with a proposal to use ground-penetrating radar to non-invasively search the suspected crash

Fig. 9.1: Two historical photographs of a portion of the Windsor Locks Army Air Field. The white star marks the area that is most consistent with eyewitness accounts of the location of Bradley's crash site. The inset is a close-up of this site, with the black arrow pointing to the suspected crash site (images courtesy of Thomas Palshaw).

site and possibly confirm its location within Bradley International Airport. The airport and CTDOT staff were agreeable to the proposal and a GPR survey was scheduled. It was assumed that the subsurface materials at the crash site would display a conspicuous cone-like structure on radar imagery. A photograph of a plane crash site that occurred on similar soil materials is shown in Figure 9.3.

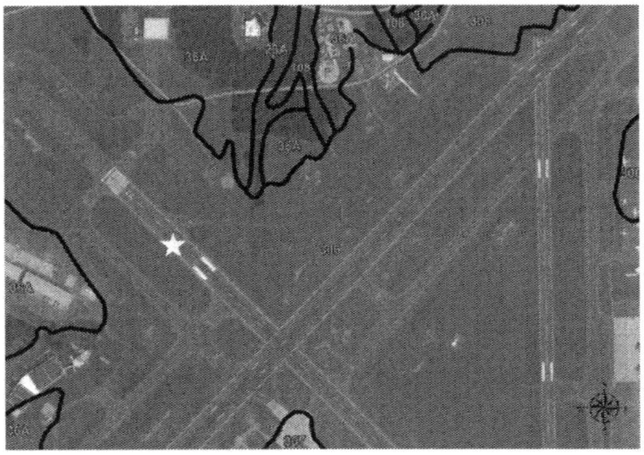

Fig. 9.2: A Web Soil Survey map of a portion of Bradley International Airport. The white star indicates the approximate location of the most credible crash site. This area, which is along the west side of Runway 15, was identified as the likely site based on the triangulation of estimated bearings to the crash from eyewitness accounts.

The suspected crash site is located on the west side of Runway 15, in an area of soils that has been mapped as unit '306': Udorthents–Urban land complex (Fig. 9.2). In Connecticut, as discussed in Chapter 7, Udorthents are

Fig. 9.3: The Bradley crash site probably had similar cone-shaped characteristics to this photograph of a plane crash site in sandy soils. Here the plane crashed 4 m (14 ft) into the ground (courtesy of Thomas Palshaw).

considered to be very deep (>1.5 m to bedrock), well-drained soils that formed in a variety of materials. Udorthents are mapped where soils have been extensively influenced, modified, or created by human activities. At airports, Udorthents typically have their topsoil removed, surface leveled (filled if necessary), and subsurface compacted. In addition, subsurface utility lines can be present. Urban land consists of soil materials that are largely covered by streets, parking lots, buildings, or, in this case, runway structures. In Connecticut, because of their generally assumed low clay, water, and soluble salt contents, Udorthents and Urban land are considered well suited for deep profiling and high resolution with GPR. Udorthents are generally considered to have high potential and Urban land is not rated for the preservation of perishable objects (Surabian 2012).

The GPR survey was conducted with a SIR-3000 control unit attached to a carry harness that was fitted around the operator's waist and shoulders. A 400 MHz antenna was systematically pulled by hand in advance of the operator and control unit (Fig. 9.4) along successive grid lines. The SIR-3000 was also connected to a Trimble GeoXH GPS through a serial data recorder (SDR) to collect synchronized GPS data.

Radar profiles collected along the grid lines were submitted to standard processing procedures of time-zero correction and background removal, with suitable color table and transform selections. The average velocity of pulse propagation and the depth scale were estimated by hyperbola matching. Because a survey wheel was not used and the data were compiled in a time mode rather than a distance mode, the collected radar data were subjected to marker editing and distance normalization procedures.

Fig. 9.4: Conducting GPR survey along a rope marked at 1 m intervals and stretched between similarly numbered chalk marks (grey arrows) on the opposing sides of the grid at Bradley International Airport (photograph courtesy of John Spaulding).

Prior to fieldwork, the suspected area of the crash site was located by measuring the angles from three known points where eye-witness observations had been made. The general area of the crash was located on Runway 15. At the suspected site, a 27 × 47 m grid area was demarcated with chalk along the runway (Fig. 9.4, arrowed). The grid's origin (0, 0) was in the south-west corner. Twenty-eight radar traverses were completed by pulling the 400 MHz antenna in a back-and-forth manner along the grid lines that were each 47 m long, orientated in a north-west to south-east direction and spaced 1 m apart. In the absence of a survey wheel, the operator impressed a mark on the radar record as the antenna was towed passed each 1 m distance mark affixed to the reference line.

Figure 9.5 contains three radar profiles from the grid site. Structurally, the profiled materials are similar on all three. The upper 1–1.5 m consist of low to moderate amplitude, horizontally layered reflection patterns. These weaky expressed, linear reflection patterns are assumed to indicate differences in the moisture content, density, and load bearing capacities of the layered base materials. The pavement surface is underlain at depths of about 15–20 cm (6–8 in) by a layer that contains a number of hyperbolically shaped point reflectors. Some of these reflection hyperbolas (yellow arrows) are underlain by reverberations, an indication of a highly reflective feature, presumably metallic. The layer that is evident at a depth of about 50 cm (20 in) contains a larger number of closely-spaced hyperbolas; perhaps indicative of some form of matting.

At depths ranging from 1–1.5 m, an undulating, moderate to high amplitude, layered reflection pattern is evident (red arrows) that stretch across the entire length of the radar profiles. It is believed that this contrasting interface represents the base of the layered, humanly-altered or humanly-transported soil materials with the upper boundary of an unstratified deposit that contains a large number of widely-spaced point reflectors (hyperbolic reflection patterns). The point reflectors are believed to represent larger rock fragments. This zone of unstratified deposits extents from depths of about 1.5 m to greater than 3 m.

The lowest structural element that is apparent on these radar profiles has an irregular upper boundary and consist of high amplitude, inclined, layered reflection patterns. These patterns are believed to represent the tilted foreset beds of sandy and gravelly, deltaic sediments that were deposited in Glacial Lake Hitchcock (Bell 1985, 196).

On all radar profiles that were collected across this grid, an anomalous cone-shaped feature is apparent running laterally for different lengths between the 0–15 m distance marks. On the profiles shown in Figure 9.5, an anomalous, cone-shaped feature is apparent between these distance marks. This feature is highlighted on each of these profiles by a green arrow. This feature is characterized by inclined, layered reflection patterns and point reflectors. After several traverses across the grid, the operator happened to notice this cone-shaped feature on one of the radar profiles. However, the extent of this feature was not apparent at the time. Because of

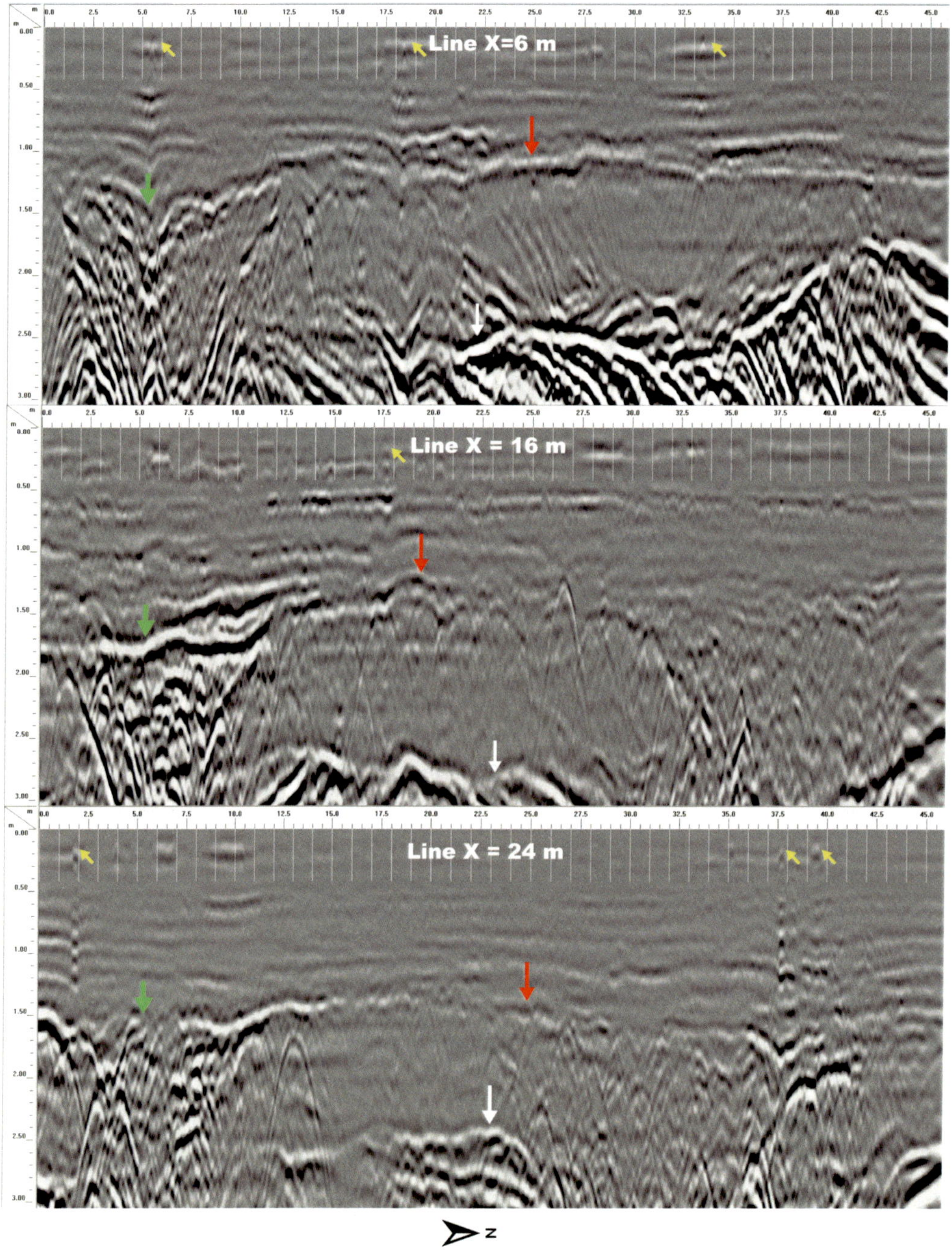

Fig. 9.5: Three representative radar profiles from the grid on Runway 15 at the Bradley International Airport.

the lack of a survey cart or wheel with an attached odometer, the operator was required to insert marks manually on the radar profile as the antenna passed each of the measured, 1 m distance marks on the reference line. In consequence, operator attention was shifted away from the console screen where the radar profiles were shown and onto the reference line. When, by happenstance, this cone-shaped feature was recognized in the field, it attracted much attention. When briefly recognized during GPR scanning, it was immediately interpreted as a refilled crater, the site of Lt Bradley's plane crash.

However, after signal processing and side-by-side review of each radar profile in the office, it became apparent that this cone-shaped feature extended across the entire width of the grid and doubts as to its identity began to arise. The reflection amplitudes, clarity, structure, and dimensions of this cone-shaped feature varied on each radar profile. In cross-section this feature was found to be approximately 10–15 m wide (32–49 ft) at its top, narrowing downwards to a depth greater than 3 m (10 ft). In Figure 9.5, note the variability in the appearance and clarity of this feature on the radar profiles. After further review and comparison of the radar profiles, it became apparent that the suspected cone-shaped crater was more akin to the structure of a refilled trench that spans a distance of over 28 m.

On the lower radar profile in Figure 9.5, reflection amplitudes are lower, suggesting greater signal attenuation at all depths as the center of Runway 15 is approached. This general weakening of the radar signals was most noticeable on the western side of the grid.

The collected GPR data from the grid site was further examined using amplitude slice-map analysis. Figure 9.6 contains four depth-slice (or time-slice) amplitude maps of the grid area. These provide a three-dimensional assessment into the location of reflection anomalies within the grid (Conyers 2013) and correspond to estimated soil depths of 15 cm, 100 cm, 200 cm, and 300 cm. For display purposes, each depth-slice amplitude image is viewed from directly overhead looking downwards into the grid.

The 15 cm depth-slice image in Figure 9.6 has a uniform, uncomplicated reflection pattern which suggest relatively similar materials. However, four sets of parallel rows that are composed of multiple, short, low amplitude, linear reflection patterns are apparent; a black dashed line has been inserted between each set of these linear reflection patterns of unknown origin.

On the 100 cm depth-slice image, four rows composed of higher amplitude, linear reflection patterns have been highlighted by black point and dash lines. These lines could represent background noise. However, this image cuts across the grid site at the approximate depth where wavy, layered reflection patterns were noted on the radar profiles in Figure 9.5. The linearity of these reflection patterns on the 100 cm depth-slice image could represent the undulating boundary of this interface or the results of subgrade stabilization and base reinforcement.

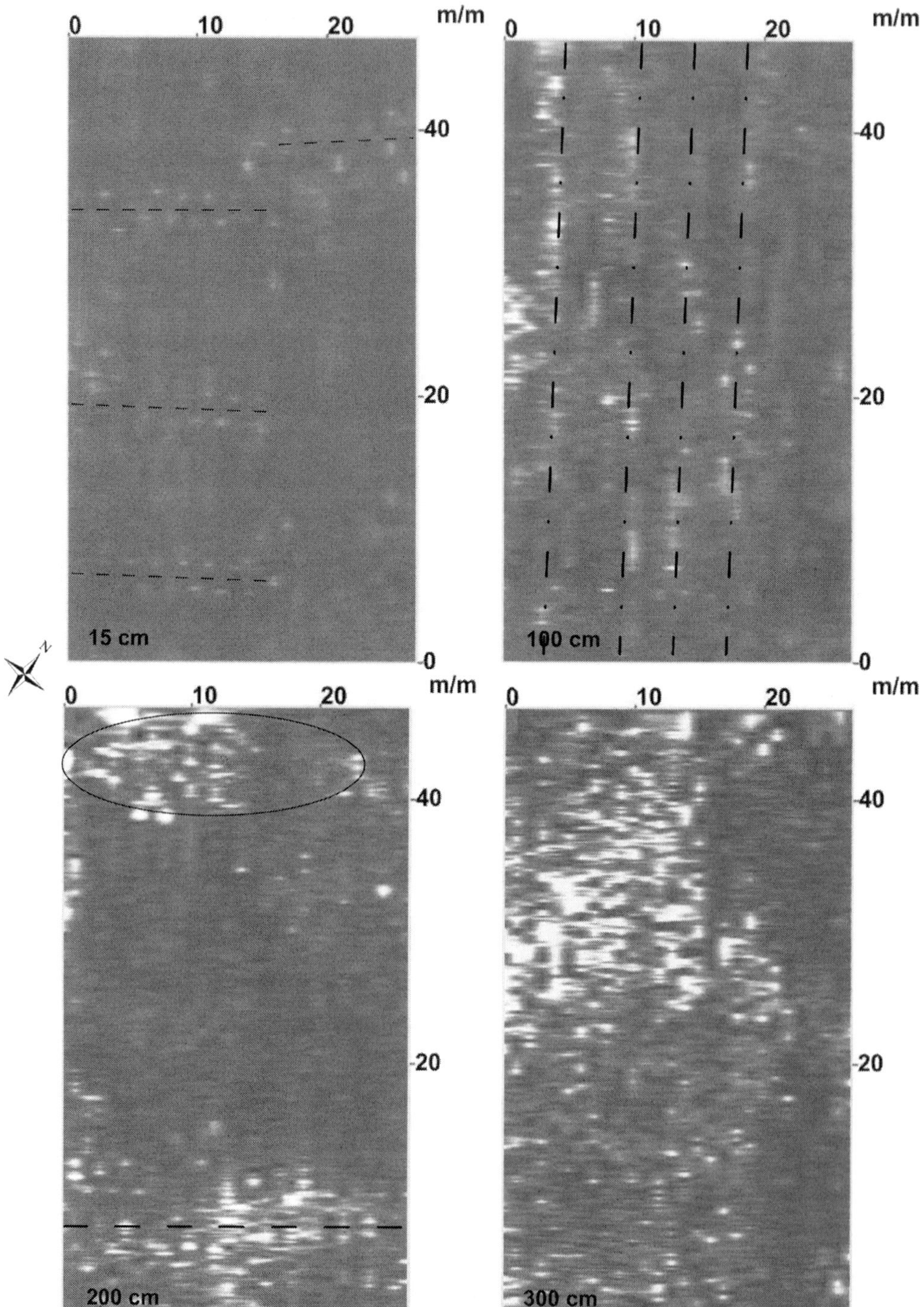

Fig. 9.6: Four depth-slice amplitude images of the grid site on Runway 15.

On the 200 cm depth-slice image, two areas with higher amplitude reflection patterns have been identified. Though ill-defined and irregularly shaped, these areas appear to stretch across most of the grid site. On this depth-slice image, the lower feature (identified by the black, dashed line) is the cone-like feature seen on the radar profiles in Figure 9.5. The upper identified area of higher amplitude reflection patterns (highlighted by the black ellipse) was not identified on the radar profiles shown in Figure 9.5 but is believed to represent the intermittent contact of the humanly altered materials with the underlying sandy and gravelly, deltaic sediments.

Higher amplitude reflection patterns on the 300 cm depth-slice image are believed to represent inhomogeneities in the underlying stratified glacial drift. These patterns are more prevalent in the north-west portion and more sporadic in other portions of the grid site. As in the other depth-slice images, reflection amplitudes appear lower in the eastern third of the grid area.

At this site, GPR provided satisfactory penetration depths and resolution of subsurface features. Radar records collected with the 400 MHz antenna were of good interpretative quality and revealed valuable subsurface information. While no subsurface feature of historical significance can be unequivocally identified on the radar images, a cone-like feature believed to be the crash site was initially identified. After the radar profiles were processed, examined more fully, and displayed in both two- and three-dimensional formats, it became apparent that the suspected feature extended across the entire grid. Because of this feature's apparent dimensions and geometry, it is presently believed, with a higher degree of interpretive certainty, to represent a refilled trench rather than a refilled crater from the crash. Design plans for Bradley Field and Bradley International Airport will have to be reviewed and state transportation officials will have to approve additional tests at the site to confirm the feature's identity.

Chapter 10

Discovering Windsor's 17th century palisade

In 1633, a group of settlers from Plymouth Plantation sailed up the Connecticut River to establish a trading house. The trading house was located near the confluence of the Connecticut with the Farmington River. They named their newly founded settlement 'Matianuck' (Howard 1935). Later, a larger group of settlers arrived in Matianuck from Dorchester, Massachusetts and excavated crude dugout shelters in the sandy banks of a nearby, prominent ridge that stretched along the north shore of the Farmington River, several hundred yards upstream from its confluence with the Connecticut River. The ridge is the first elevated ground above the western bank of the Connecticut River floodplain.[1] They would name their settlement 'Dorchester' after the town that they had left. Following the outbreak of the Pequot War, these settlers abandoned their dugouts on the side slopes of the sandy ridge and congregated on the ridge top in an area that is now known as the Palisado Green (Howard 1935).

During the Pequot War (1636–1638), many Connecticut plantations had their homes fortified and surrounded by a picket palisade. These palisades were constructed of sturdy timbers that were set upright, side-by-side, in the ground. Settlers living within these picket walls would temporarily provide portions of their home lots to accommodate additional refugee families that had moved into the palisade for protection. In 1637, Dorchester was enclosed in a palisade, or palisado, to protect the settlement from the hostile Pequots. It was during the Pequot War that the settlers at Dorchester renamed their settlement to 'Windsor'. The Windsor palisade was rhomboid in shape with a perimeter that measured approximately 4300 ft (*c.* 1310 m). A wide ditch was dug outside this palisade with the excavated soil materials thrown against the picket walls (Howard 1935). Based on historical records, a major portion of the palisade is known to have extended from the southwest corner of the old burying ground, east-south-east along the Farmington River, then north-east along the ridge's upper cusp (Fig. 10.1). The Windsor palisade was reportedly removed by 1640.[2]

In 1640, Windsor's Town Clerk, Mathew Grant, compiled a map that listed the homeowners, their land, and the location of the palisade walls. Drawing from Grant's map, Henry Stiles produced a similar map in 1891 (Fig. 10.1), which was included in his book *History and Genealogies of Ancient Windsor*. In this book, Stiles mentions the location of the still visible remnants of the palisade's ditch:

> This south line was 60 rods [1155 ft/350 m] long; and along the south side of the passage leading from the meeting-house to the burying-ground are now [1891] to be seen the remains of a ditch, believed to have been a part of the south line of the fortification. (Stiles 1891, 136).

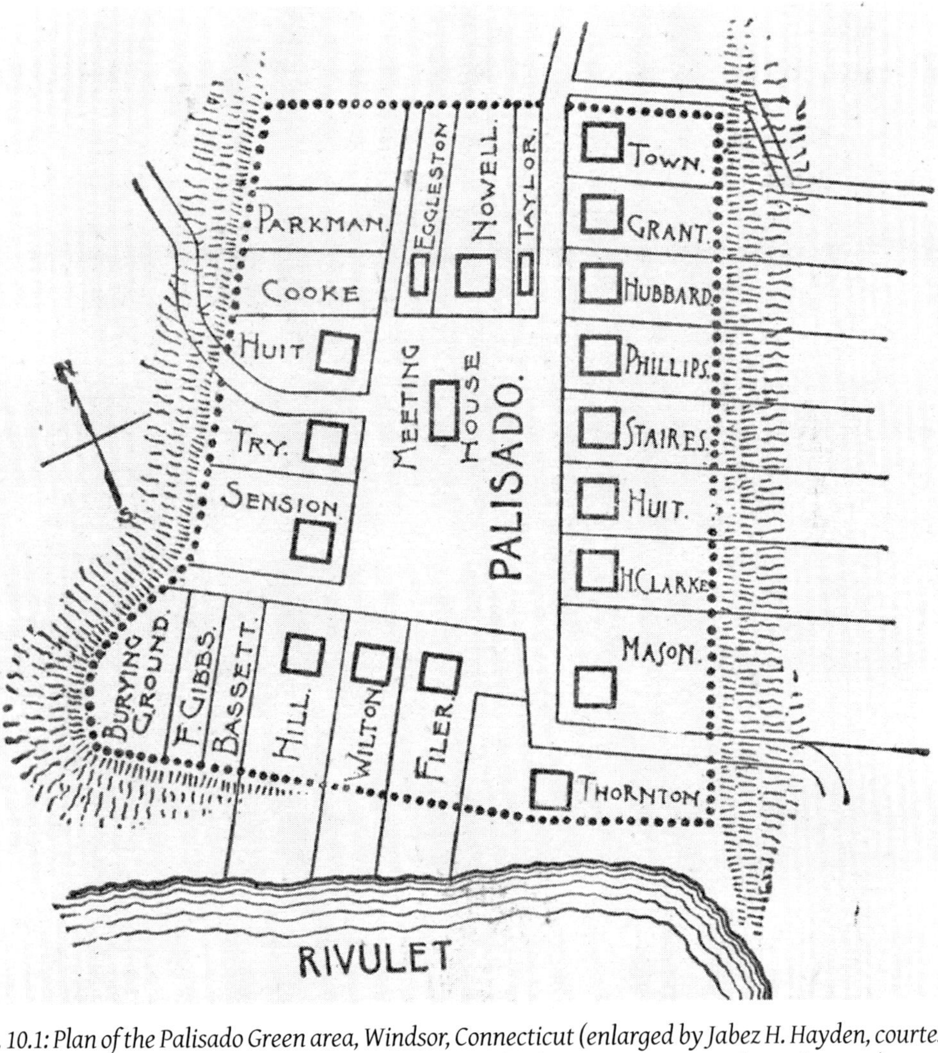

Fig. 10.1: Plan of the Palisado Green area, Windsor, Connecticut (enlarged by Jabez H. Hayden, courtesy of the publishers of The Memorial History of Hartford County, *as printed in Stiles 1891).*

Since the publication of Stiles' book, attempts have been made to find remnants of the Windsor palisade. In the 1980s and 1990s, several unsuccessful test pits and trenches were excavated in efforts to uncover evidence for it (Trocchi 2007). As noted by Trocchi (2007): 'Evidence of the Palisade's remains would be a wonderful accomplishment, no matter how small a feature that is found'. In 2005, a GPR survey was conducted across two residential lawns in Windsor that, according to historic records, were likely occupied by the palisade. The purpose of this survey was to identify anomalous, subsurface features on radar imagery that suggested potential evidence of the palisade wall and former structures that were built within its circuit.

The investigated sites are located about 0.5 mile (0.8 km) north-east of the center of Windsor. Prior to conducting the GPR investigation, a soil map from the Web Soil Survey was reviewed to determine the relative suitability of soil conditions at the selected sites for GPR. Grids 1 and 2 are located within soil delineations that are labeled '34A' and '234B', respectively (white boxes on Fig. 10.2). These symbols identify the soil map units as Merrimac fine sandy loam on 0–3% slopes (34A) and Merrimac-Urban land complex on 0–8% slopes (234B). The very deep (>1.5 m to bedrock), somewhat excessively drained, Merrimac soils formed in gravelly and sandy

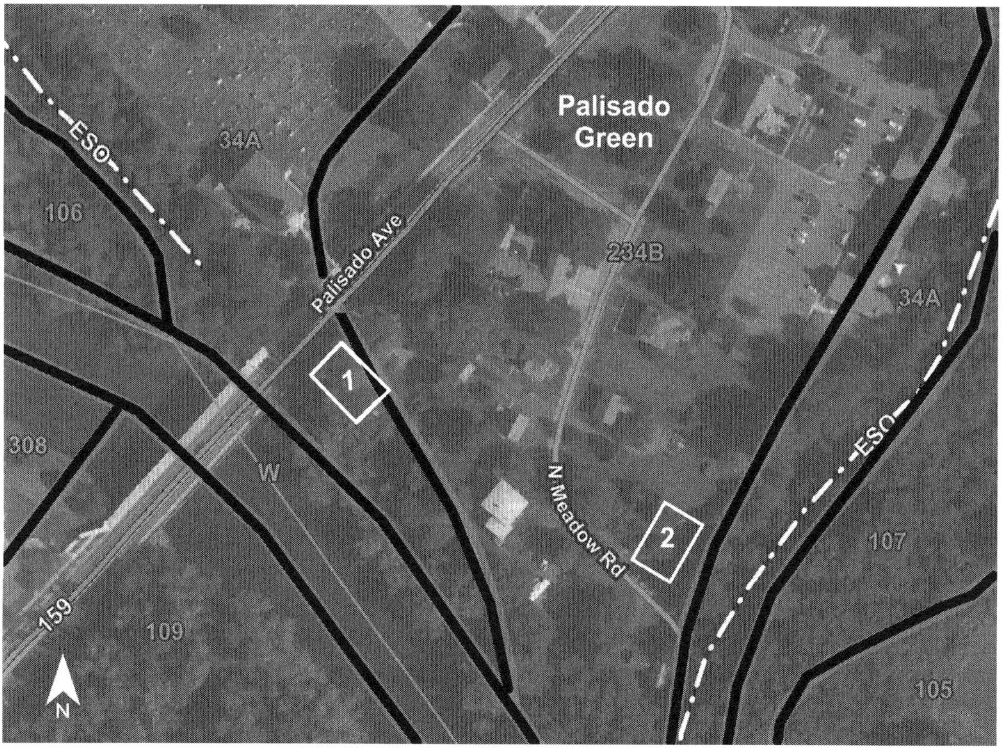

Fig. 10.2: This Web Soil Survey map shows the soils mapped in the area of the former Windsor Palisade. The white rectangles indicate the approximate locations of the GPR survey grids.

outwash deposits. The Merrimac soils have solums (A, AE, E, Bw, and/or BC horizons) that typically range in thickness from about 45 cm to 90 cm (18–36 in) with rock fragment contents that can range from 2% to 30%. The substratum is stratified and has a rock fragment content that ranges from 2% to 70%. Because Merrimac soils contain less than 18% clay and lack free water and soluble salts, they have relatively low electrical conductivities and are considered well suited to GPR. Urban land represents a miscellaneous area that is mostly covered by streets, parking lots, and buildings (see description in Chapter 7) and, in Connecticut, are considered generally well suited to GPR. In Figure 10.2, the line labelled 'ESO' identifies the location of a narrow, continuous, steep escarpment.

This study was conducted over soils that are considered well suited to deep profiling and high resolution with GPR. However, in these soils any wooden object, such as the timbers that composed the palisado walls, will decompose rapidly over time as a result of microbial decay and non-biological degradation processes. The moderately acid to extremely acid soil reaction and the free-draining nature of Merrimac soils create conditions that hasten the deterioration of buried wooden materials and artifacts (Surabian 2012). In Merrimac and similar soils, wooden objects and artifacts have been observed to decay rapidly and disintegrate over time leaving little or no evidence of their presence to be detected with GPR. Point anomalies (i.e., rock fragments, larger tree roots) and strata within the gravelly and sandy outwash deposits can produce high level of unwanted noise and clutter which can obscure reflections from desired targets and foster uncertainties and restrain interpretations.

In this GPR investigation, a 10 × 19.6 m grid was established across each site which, based on historical records, was identified as a likely location of the former palisade. Both sites consist of level lawns that are bordered by trees (Figs 10.2, 10.3). Using standard field procedures and a 50 cm grid line interval, radar traverses were completed along parallel grid lines in a back-and-forth manner. The traverse (grid) lines were 10 m and 19.6 m long for grids 1 and 2, respectively. Radar traverses were conducted with the SIR-3000 control unit attached to a carry harness that was fitted to the operator. A 400 MHz antenna provided suitable investigation depth and resolution of subsurface features in the two areas of Merrimac soils. A survey wheel was attached to the antenna (Fig. 10.3).

All radar profiles were submitted to standard processing procedures of time-zero correction and background removal, with suitable color table and transform selections. For each site, a three-dimensional data volume of the assembled radar profiles was constructed and horizontally sliced at difference depths to provide a top-down view of the data. The average velocity of pulse propagation and the depth scale were estimated by hyperbola matching.

Figure 10.4 contains two representative radar profiles from Grid 1. A noticeable contrast in reflection patterns distinguishes the soil solum (A and Bw horizons) from substratum (2C horizon). On the radar profiles the contact separating these two distinct layers ranges in depth from about 55 cm to 90 cm along the X = 2 m line

Fig. 10.3: A portion of Grid 1 showing the 400 MHz antennae with an attached survey wheel. In the background is the Palisado Avenue Bridge, which spans the Farmington River on State Route 159.

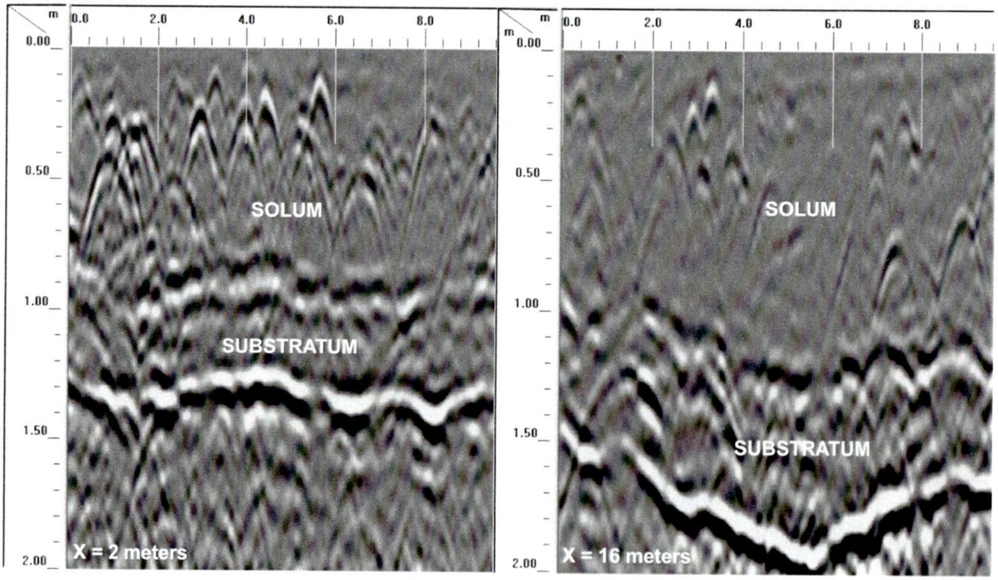

Fig. 10.4: Representative radar profiles from lines X = 2 m and X = 16 m of Grid 1.

and from about 85 cm to 120 cm along the X = 16 m line. On both radar profiles, the solum is composed of scattered point reflectors with an absence of layered reflection patterns. The lack of noticeable, layered reflection patterns in the solum suggest relatively homogenous materials and the absence of highly contrasting soil horizons (see Fig. 10.5). The substratum is composed of two distinct, layered reflection patterns each having a wavy topography. The upper layered reflection pattern (i.e., contact between solum and substratum) appears more segmented and weakly expressed than the lower layered reflection pattern (i.e., contact between different outwash strata). This suggests the presence of a gradual or transitional boundary separating the solum from the substratum.

On the radar profiles shown in Figure 10.4, point reflectors are distinguished by their hyperbolic reflection patterns. The majority of the point reflectors appear to occur within the upper 50 cm (20 in) of the soil profile. Across this portion of both radar profiles, the distribution of point reflectors varies both in numbers and reflection amplitudes. This portion of the profiles represents our area of interest, as any signs of the suspected palisade wall, or other historic structures or layers would likely be embedded within these depths. The concentration of hyperbolas within these depths could be interpreted as a sign of the formerly embedded picket wall. However, the strong amplitudes of these hyperbolas suggests a more recent, less decayed, feature. The two survey flags highlighted by white arrows in Figure 10.3 mark the northern and southern end points of radar profile X = 2 m in Figure 10.4. As two large trees occur within a short distance of this traverse line, it was assumed likely that some of the point reflectors evident on the radar profile represent larger tree roots. Other point reflectors could represent larger rock fragments, animal burrows, or soil inhomogeneities, as well as buried artifacts. While the GPR has distinguished these point anomalies, uncertainties exist as to their identities.

Fig. 10.5: Soil excavation completed in Grid 1. The black dashed line indicates the boundary that separates the solum from the substratum. Black arrows indicate the broken ends of larger tree roots.

Figure 10.5 shows an archaeological test pit that was opened along a portion of line X = 2 m in Grid 1. The major soil horizons (A, Bw, 2C) of a Merrimac soil profile are well expressed on this image. The broken ends of several large roots (black arrows) and many smaller roots are evident in the portion of the solum exposed along the sidewall of the excavation. A black, dashed line has been inserted to mark the approximate contact of the solum with the underlying substratum.

The GPR data that was collected from Grid 1 was examined using amplitude slice-map analysis. Figure 10.6 illustrates six time-slice (or depth-slice) amplitude images of the grid. These provide top-down, planar views of the soil at projected depths of 0 cm, 15 cm, 30 cm, 50 cm, 75 cm, and 100 cm.

On the 15 cm and 30 cm depth-slice images, a white arrow has been used to identify a shallowly buried, linear feature that extends across the entirety of the grid and represents the most noticeable and significant feature that can be discerned on these images. This feature closely follows the banks to the Farmington River, which is located to the south. This reflection pattern was identified as a feature of interest. Although a high degree of uncertainty was placed on this interpretation as being possible remnants of the 17th century palisade, this linear anomaly provided archaeologists with a clue as to where to strategically locate a test pit. Figure 10.7 is a photograph of the excavated test pit, showing roots in the foreground and two cable lines (black arrows) in the background. No remnants of a palisade wall were identified in this exposure.

On the 0 cm, 15 cm, and 30 cm depth-slice images, a low amplitude, linear feature has been identified by a black arrow. Though weakly expressed, this linear feature appears to become more prominent and longer with increasing soil depth on these

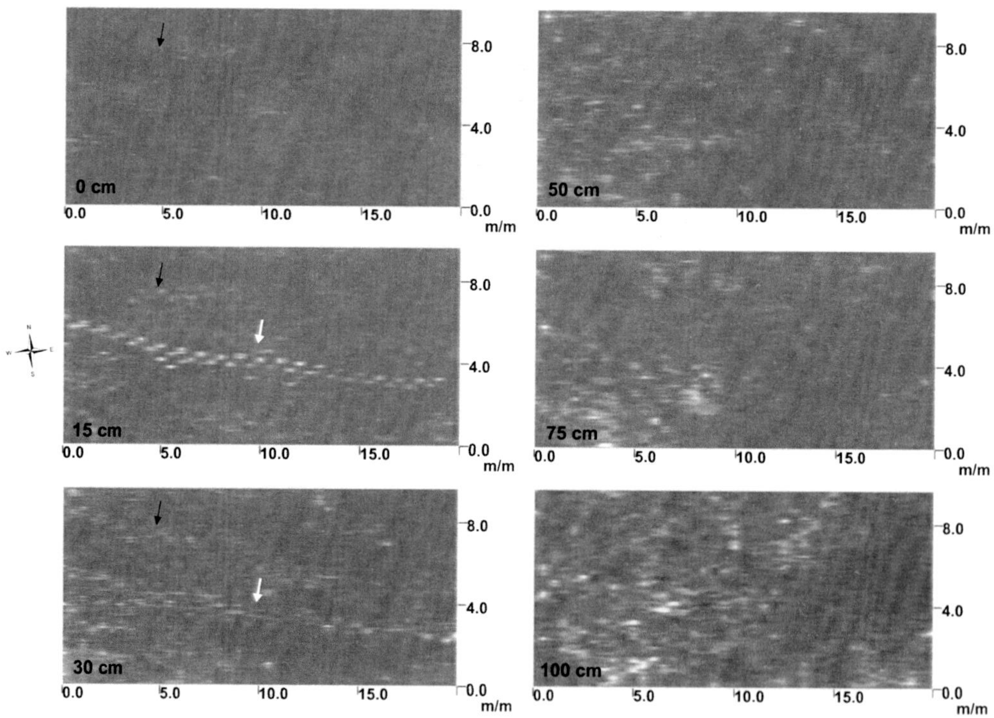

Fig. 10.6: Six depth-slice amplitude images of Grid 1.

three images. It was associated with larger, closely spaced tree roots in the test pit.

Moderate to high amplitude point reflection patterns are evident on most depth-slice amplitude images shown in Figure 10.6. These reflection patterns increase in both amplitude and number with increasing depth. On the 15 cm and 30 cm depth-slice images, the point reflections have low amplitudes and appear amassed mainly along the western and southern borders of the grid. By their locations, these reflection patterns were principally attributed to the larger roots of trees that border this area of the grid (see Fig. 10.3). On the 75 cm and 100 cm depth-slice images, the moderate to high amplitude reflection patterns that appear to spread out across the grid from the south-west corner were attributed to the irregular contact of the solum with the underlying substratum and the likely occurrence of larger rock fragments.

Fig. 10.7: An archaeological dig confirming the identity of the shallow linear features highlighted by white arrows in the 15 cm depth-slice amplitude image of Fig. 10.6 as two cable lines.

Figure 10.8 contains three representative radar profiles from Grid 2. As on the exhibited radar profiles from Grid 1 (Fig. 10.4), these display a major contrast in reflection patterns that distinguishes the soil solum from substratum. However, in Grid 2, this contact appears to decrease in reflection amplitudes and becomes more obscure with each succeeding traverse across the grid (3–6–9 m). On these three radar profiles, this contact ranges in depth from about 60 cm to 100 cm. The solum is represented by a number of point reflectors having widely varying reflection amplitudes and lacks noticeable layered reflection patterns. The substratum consists of stratified, layered reflection patterns. Knowing that Merrimac soils formed in water deposited sediments, these reflection patterns were divided into topset (white arrow) and foreset (black arrow) grouping patterns. The uppermost topset reflection pattern forms the contact between solum and substratum. In general, the reflection patterns that form the topset beds are weakly expressed and have a more irregular topography than the lower, more steeply inclined, layered reflection patterns of the foreset beds. On the radar profiles in Figure 10.8, a black arrow identifies the contact between topset and foreset beds.

In Figure 10.8, on the radar profiles from the 6 m and 9 m grid lines, a rectangular area, highlighted by dashed, black lines, has been recognized. This area contains

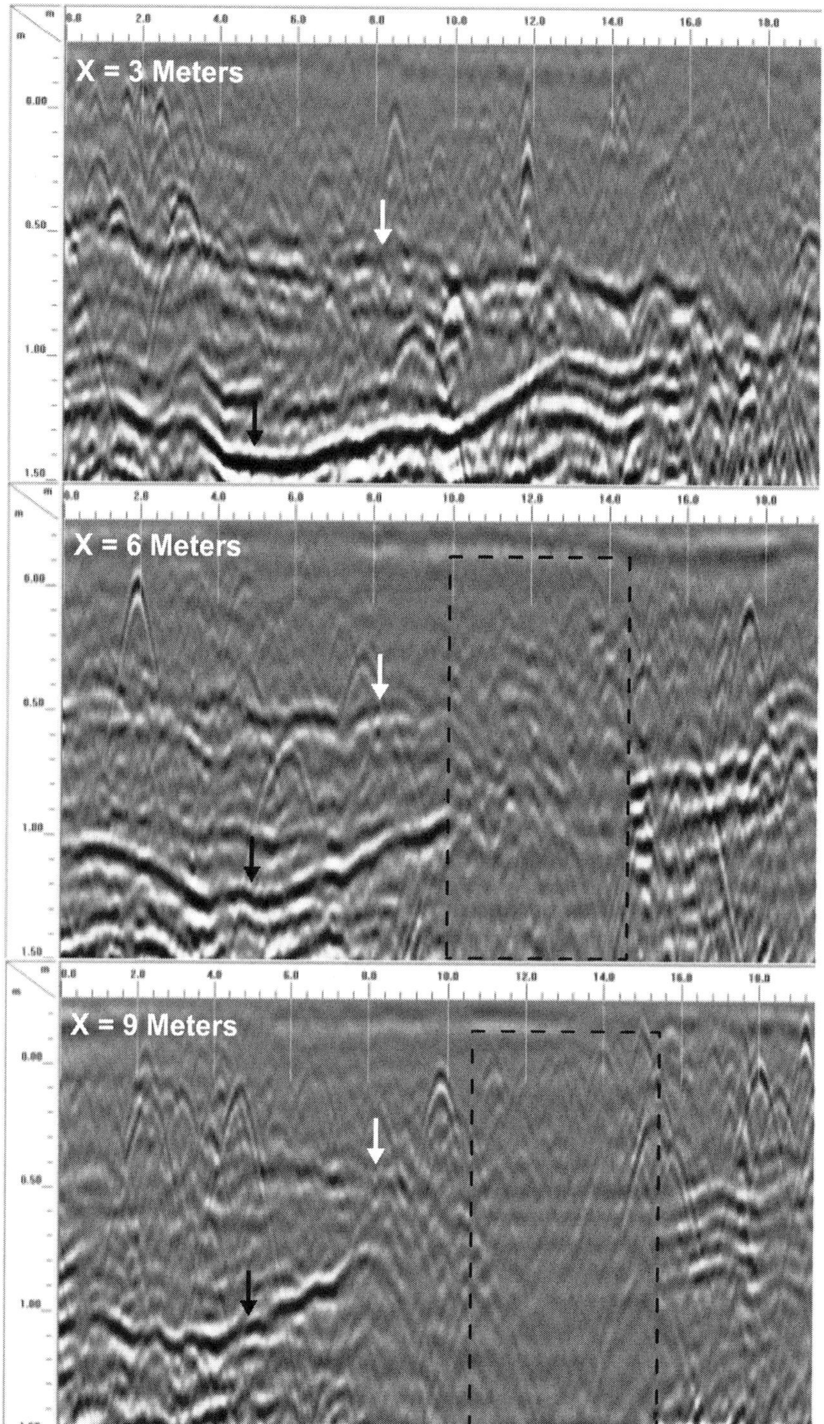

Fig. 10.8: Representative radar profiles from Grid 2, lines X = 3 m, 6 m, and 9 m.

noticeable signs of signal attenuation and contrasting reflection patterns, and appears to extend from the soil surface to the maximum profiling depth of 1.5 m. The rather abrupt truncation of adjoining soil and stratigraphic features, dissimilar reflection patterns, and the absence of higher-amplitude reflections, suggest an area of soil disturbance and/or possible contamination.

Figure 10.9 contains six depth-slice amplitude images from Grid 2. Each image provides a top-down, planar view of the soil at projected depths of 0 cm, 15 cm, 30 cm, 50 cm, 75 cm, and 100 cm. With an increase in soil depth, there is an increase in the number of moderate and high amplitude reflections (colored gray and white, respectively), especially at depths of 50 cm or greater. Also, with an increase in depth, reflection patterns change from few and predominantly point, to numerous, with both point and layered reflection patterns aggregated into broad bands.

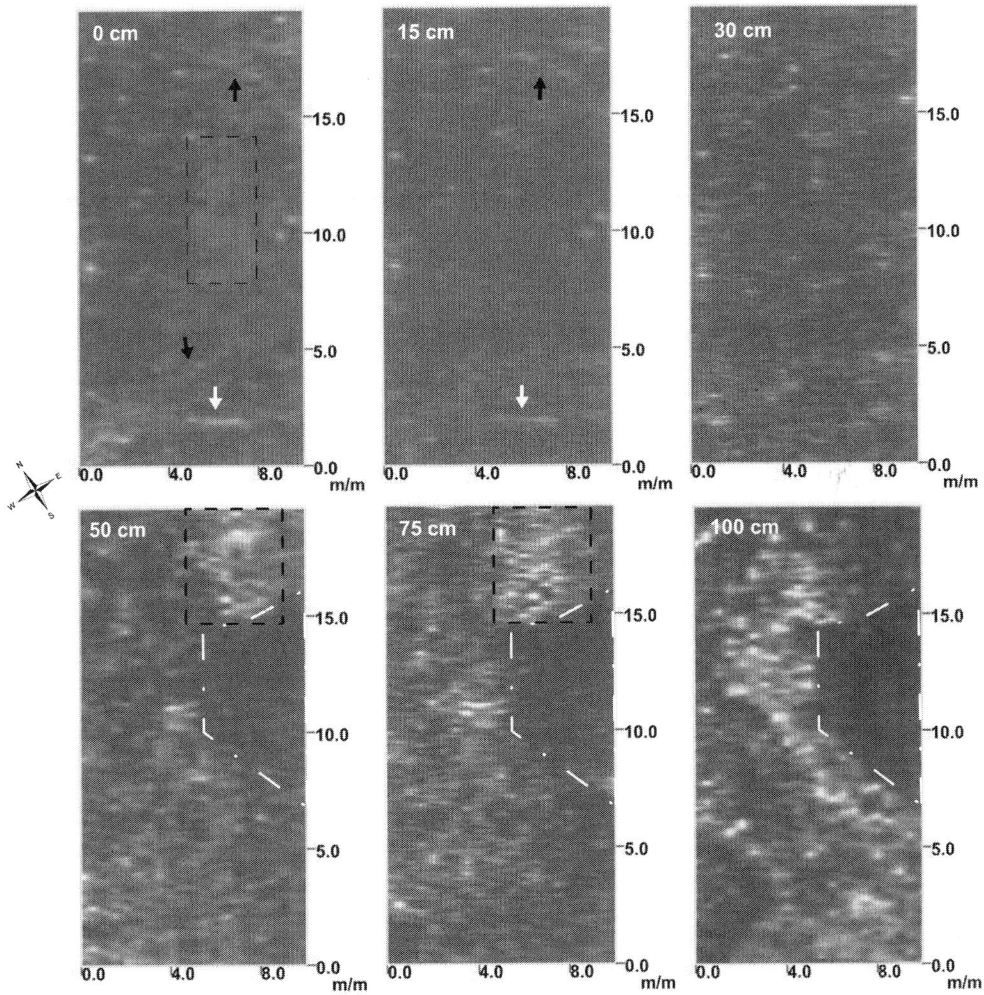

Fig. 10.9: Six depth-slice amplitude images from Grid 2.

The shallow, 0 cm and 15 cm depth-slice amplitude images contain a number of widely-dispersed point reflectors. After over 375 years of known use and occupation of the area, many of these point anomalies likely represent discarded artifacts. A weakly-expressed rectangular feature and several low to moderate amplitude linear features of possible significance have been identified on these two depth-slice images. The weakly-expressed rectangular feature that is outlined on the 0 cm depth-slice image could represent a figment of the imagination, a repatched section of the lawn, or, possibly, an area of former settlement or use history. Three, short, linear anomalies have been identified on these images. A white arrow has been used to identify a prominent linear anomaly located in an area of the grid that is most likely to contain remnants of the former palisade. In addition, the orientation of this linear anomaly parallels the course of the Farmington River. The black arrows identify two, more weakly-expressed, curvilinear features that may be of historical significance.

On the 50 cm and 75 cm depth-slice amplitude images shown in Figure 10.9, a rectangular-shaped area containing a large concentration of high-amplitude reflections has been enclosed by dashed black lines. This relatively large, area was interpreted as an area of disturbance and, possibly, a refilled cellar. A subtle, but noteworthy, change in reflection patterns for this area can be seen on the 2D radar profile that was completed along line X = 6 m in Figure 10.8. Following this GPR investigation, archaeologists excavated a test pit at this location, and unearthed numerous 18th century artifacts, along with some that have been dated back to the 1600s (Fig. 10.10).

Fig. 10.10: Test pit completed in Grid 2. The base of this excavation approximates the contact separating natural soil layers below from humanly transported and altered materials above.

A large area of 'no signal return' is evident on the 50 cm, 75 cm, and 100 cm depth-slice amplitude images shown in Figure 10.9. This area has been outlined by the segment, white lines of a polygon. This area, which is located on the eastern side of the grid, was also noted on two of the three radar profiles shown in Figure 10.6. Radar profiles from this area have noticeable signal attenuation and contrasting reflection patterns. However, the reason(s) for this area of increased attenuation remains unknown.

The GPR investigation at these locations in Windsor did not verify the former existence, nor the location, of the palisade. However, radar profiles and depth-slice imagery did expose several areas of interest where archaeological excavations were focused. Radar profiles collected at these sites revealed the structural architecture of the Merrimac soil. However, the large number of point anomalies in the profiled soils, obscured the identification of reflections from the 17th century palisade, if any significant reflections are still possible. At Grid 1, depth-sliced amplitude imagery revealed two linear features, which extended across the entire grid site parallel with the banks of the Farmington River, and in a likely location for the former palisade. These clues led archaeologists to excavate a trench in which the anomalous features were identified as two cable lines. At Grid 2, several short, very shallow, linear anomalies were identified. Some or all of these features may be of historical significance. At deeper soil depths, two anomalous areas were identified: one was interpreted as an area of soil disturbance, possibly the site of a historical structure; and one was interpreted as an area of significant signal attenuation, which was assumed to be caused by the physical and chemical composition of soil materials. A test pit in the former area revealed a mantle of humanly-transported and altered materials in which a significant number of mostly 18th century artifacts were unearthed. This test pit also revealed artifacts dating back to the 1600s.

Notes

1 https://www.livingplaces.com/CT/Hartford_County/Windsor_Town/Palisado_Avenue_Historic_District.html
2 https://windsorhistoricalsociety.org/windsor-history/

Chapter 11

Elijah Welles homestead, Newington

Wethersfield, which was founded by English emigrants along the western bank of the Connecticut River in 1634, is considered the earliest permanent colonial settlement in the state, though a trading post had been erected a year earlier in Windsor to the north at the confluence of the Farmington River (see Chapter 10). Survival was tenuous for the incipient villagers, especially when Wethersfield residents soon found themselves under siege by the Pequot Nation. In a surprise attack on the morning of 23 April 1637, Pequot warriors emerged out of the woods and killed nine farmers while they tended their fields and took two young Wethersfield girls as captives. Fortunately, the captive girls were later ransomed by Dutch traders and returned to their families. With a colonial victory ending the Pequot War (1636–1637) and population increases, the riverine-based colony expanded westward into the uplands of present-day Newington, Connecticut, searching for additional farmland.

Beginning in 1670, a series of mile-wide (0.8 km) lots were granted near Wethersfield's western frontier with Farmington, Connecticut. The appointed Wethersfield men who would determine the division of this land into property lots and their distribution among Wethersfield families included Capt. Robert Welles and Sgt Jonathan Welles, both veterans of the Pequot War. One of the recipients of a 26 × 442 rods (429 × 7293 ft; about 72 acres/29 ha) tract of land was 'Capt. Weels' or Capt. Robert Welles himself (Baxter 1971, 17). By the turn of the 18th century, while farms were being cleared, the recent settlers were experiencing difficulties travelling over the steep basalt ridge during winter months in order to attend church services and town meetings in Wethersfield center. To ease these hardships, a permanent church was granted for the winter months of 1709.

Originally called the 'West Society of Wethersfield', the new settlement soon became familiarly known as 'Newington Society' and 'West Farms'. Though the farmland was good, especially for pasturing, the adversity of having to travel over poor roads that crossed the steeply inclined basalt ridge once again proved too much and the new community got off to a slow start, remaining an extension of Wethersfield until the late 19th century. By commencement of the American Revolutionary War (1776), Newington Society had 500 residents, almost exclusively farmers.

In 1871, the occupants of the Newington Society successfully petitioned the Connecticut General Assembly for incorporation as a separate town. The author of the measure for incorporation was Roger Welles. Hence, the Welles family (also spelled 'Wells' and 'Weels') played a significant role in the history of Newington from its first division to its incorporation and into the 20th century.

Elijah Welles was born in October 1744, married Sarah Kellogg in November of 1772 in Wethersfield (presumably Newington), lived in a large saltbox house on a hill along the district's main north–south road (Fig. 11.1) and farmed the land until his death in May 1811 at the age of 66 years. Elijah and Sarah would raise six children in their Main Street home.

The present inhabitants of the historic Elijah Welles house (*c.* 1774) have repeatedly noticed faint, linear patterns within their backyard, especially as winter snows melt away. An exploratory excavation near the approximate location of one of these lines revealed brick and stone works (Fig. 11.2). Interested by these findings, the homeowners contacted the Connecticut State Archaeologist and requested a

Fig. 11.1: The Elijah Welles House on Main Street, Newington, Connecticut.

Fig. 11.2: An excavation in the backyard of the Welles House revealed buried stonework.

more appropriate and comprehensive archaeological investigation of the backyard. As the area to be investigated was rather large, a preliminary ground-penetrating radar investigation was proposed to possibly discover the presence of other buried historical features, decrease search time and costs, and, if needed, facilitate future excavation strategies.

Based on historical documents, pictures of the site, and observations made by the property's owners, a survey grid was established across a portion of the Welles house's backyard. This grid was established over a soil delineation that is labeled '228B', which denotes an area of Elmridge-Urban land complex on 0–8% slopes (Fig. 11.3). Elmridge is a very deep (>1.5 m to bedrock), moderately well drained soil that formed in loamy over clayey sediments on glacial lacustrine and marine terraces. Depth to the underlying, clayey sediments (2C horizon) typically ranges from 46 cm to 102 cm (18–40 in). In places, the 2C horizons can contain strata of course-textured materials. Because of the higher clay content of the 2C horizons, Elmridge soils are considered only moderately suited to deep profiling with GPR. It was anticipated, however, that any historical feature of interest would be buried within the overlying, loamy solum and detectable with GPR. Areas of Urban land consist of grounds that are covered by pavement, buildings, and other impervious, humanly-manufactured surfaces and structures. Underlying these impermeable layers and structures are artificially altered or transported earthen materials, natural soil materials, or a mix of both.

Fig. 11.3: A soil map showing the location of the GPR grid survey (white, dashed lines) behind the Welles House.

Urban land can exhibit a wide range of poorly characterized physical and chemical properties that impact the effectiveness of GPR.

A 14 × 23 m grid was established across an open, lawn area located behind the Welles' house (dashed rectangle on Fig. 11.3). Two parallel boundary lines were laid out forming the eastern and western sides of the proposed grid area. Along these lines, survey flags were inserted in the ground at 50 cm intervals. Parallel traverses were completed with the radar unit along a guide rope, which was stretched between similarly numbered flags on the opposing boundary lines (Fig. 11.4). The rope was uniformly marked at intervals of 1 m. The radar traverses were conducted across the grid area in back-and-forth manner along grid lines orientated in a general east–west direction. A total of 29, 23 m long radar traverses were conducted along these grid lines.

The GPR survey was completed using a SIR-3000 data acquisition system with a 400 MHz antenna. Neither the GPR survey cart nor survey wheel was available for this survey. As a consequence, the setup on the SIR-3000 control unit was programmed

Fig. 11.4: Conducting the GPR grid survey at the Welles House.

to a time-based mode of operation. Time-based radar data contains no distance identifiers. In the time-based mode, the antenna is moved along the surface at a steady speed, and user marks are inserted in the collected radar data at each measured distance mark along the traverse line. During the post-processing, the time-based radar data are submitted to a distance normalization procedure, which establishes a constant distance scale between the inserted user marks. During post-processing, all the radar data were submitted to standard processing procedures of time-zero correction and background removal, with suitable color table and transform selections. The average velocity of pulse propagation and the depth scale were estimated by hyperbola matching.

A representative portion of a radar profile from the grid site is shown in Figure 11.5. This profile shows the first 15 m of the radar traverse that was conducted along grid line X = 5 m. On this profile, both the depth and distance scales are expressed in meters. The white and dark arrows shown in the upper portion of this radar profile are believed to identify reflections from scattered cultural debris (e.g., bricks, pipes, tools, and shards of glass and pottery) and buried foundations, respectively. As Elmridge soils lack larger rock fragments and this traverse line was distant from trees and their projected rooting systems, the point reflectors evident on this radar profile were attributed to buried cultural features. The reflections from the inferred buried foundations (dark arrows) appear larger,

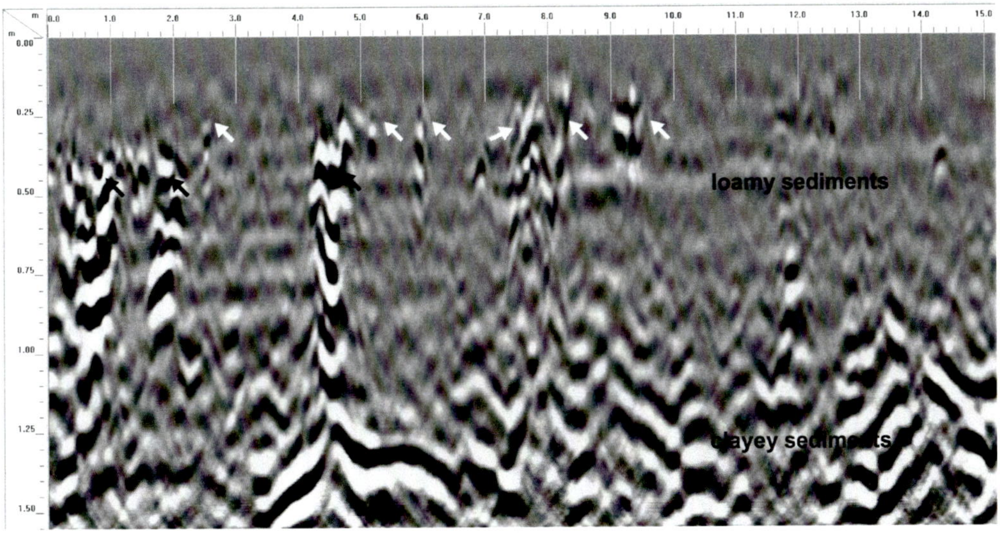

Fig. 11.5: A representative portion of a radar profile from the GPR grid survey at the Welles House.

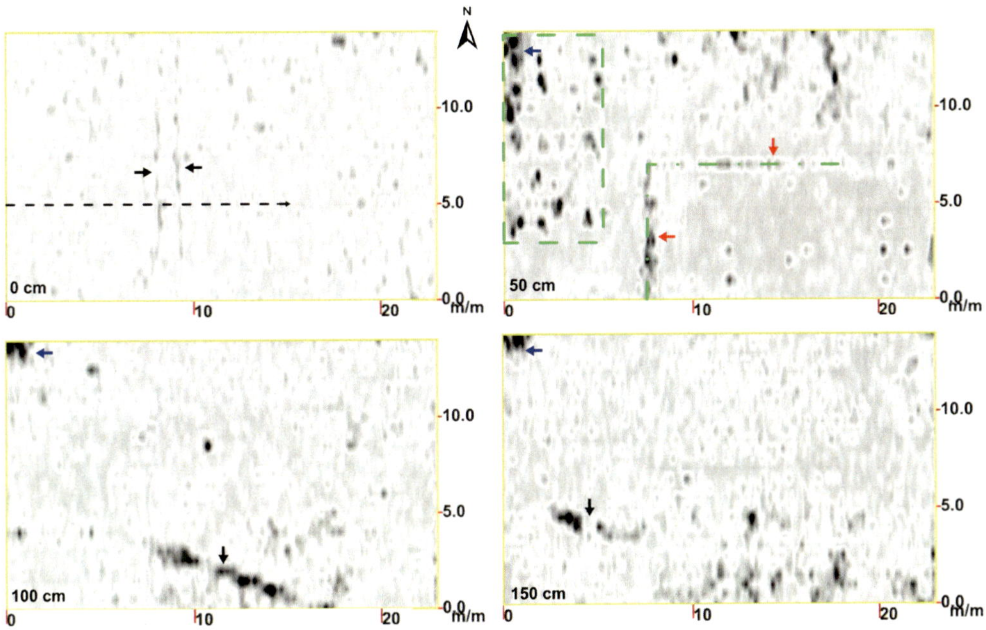

Fig. 11.6: Four depth-slice amplitude images from the Welles GPR grid survey.

have an underlying sequence of multiple reflections that extend to greater depths, and higher signal amplitudes than the reflections (white arrows) from the likely scattered cultural debris, which would be noticeably smaller and have slightly lower signal amplitudes.

Except for the aforementioned point anomalies, the overlying loamy solum is nondescript and contains only faint indications of soil horizonation (A and Bw horizons). A continuous, though weakly expressed and highly variable, layered reflection pattern occurs at depths ranging from 10 cm to 25 cm (4–10 in). This layered reflection pattern could represent the contact separating the A and Bw horizons, or slight differences in soil density, texture, or moisture contents. Additional, weakly expressed, layered reflection patterns occur within the solum, but are truncated by the strong reflection from the aforementioned point reflectors.

In the radar profile appearing in Figure 11.5, the clayey sediments, which compose the substratum of the Elmridge soils, appear as strongly expressed, layered reflection patterns. The boundary that separates the clayey (2C horizons) from the overlying loamy (A and Bw horizons) sediments is highly irregular and poorly defined. While this boundary occurs between depths of about 0.75 m and 1.25 m, it is difficult to trace laterally on the radar profile. The layered, clayey sediments have a broken to irregular topography, which appears to be thrusted upwards, towards the west (left side of this profile).

Figure 11.6 contains four depth-slice amplitude images of the grid area providing a cross-sectional view at soil depths of about 0 cm, 50 cm, 100 cm, and 150 cm. For display purposes, each depth-slice amplitude image is viewed from directly overhead looking downwards into the grid.

On the 0 cm depth-slice amplitude image, the black, dashed, horizontal line represents the location of the radar profile shown in Figure 11.5. This depth-slice image contains many scattered point reflectors and two thin, parallel, weakly-expressed, linear reflection patterns. The two linear reflectors extend across most of the grid area in a general north–south direction. These lines have been identified by two black arrows. These linear reflectors are spaced about 1 m apart. It is likely that these reflectors produced the patterns that were observed by the property owners as the winter snow cover melted away. The shallow depth and appearance of these reflectors suggest the boundaries of a former walkway.

In the upper left-hand corner of the 50 cm, 100 cm, and 150 cm depth-slice images, a blue arrow indicates the location of a recurring, high amplitude reflection pattern. This occurs next to the buried stonework shown in Figure 11.2. As such, this reflection pattern was attributed to the continuation of this stonework.

On the 50 cm depth-slice amplitude image, dashed, green lines have been inserted to emphasize reflections that are believed to represent buried structural features. The two dashed, green lines that are identified with red arrows directly lie on top of two, orthogonally intersecting, linear features that were interpreted as representing buried, foundation walls. The dashed, green lines in the mid- to upper, left-hand corner of the grid identify multiple reflection patterns whose overall appearance suggests the remnants of a large former structural feature.

On the 100 cm and 150 cm depth-slice images, black arrows have been used to identify portions of an elongated, linear feature. While more extensive on the

100 cm image, the continuation of this feature on the 150 cm image is apparent. With succeeding (deeper) depth-slices, this buried feature appears to extend in a west-north-westerly direction towards the Welles' house, which is located to the west (left-hand side) of the grid site.

Several line or random walk GPR traverses were conducted across the remaining portions of the backyard. These revealed a single, conspicuous subsurface reflection pattern on several radar profiles. This pattern is located near the house and was interpreted as representing an abandoned well. Limited excavations disclosed another subsurface brickwork feature.

The GPR survey highlighted the below-ground remnants of the Welles farming complex. New England farms necessitated the need for many ancillary structures, from barns, sheds, storage facilities, animal penning, and even seasonal blacksmithing and carpentry operations. These multi-occupational activities play out in physical need for temporary structures, the extent of which is rarely seen in standing buildings. Yet, hidden under the ground in artifacts and foundation features, we can find the traces of important pieces of New England history.

Chapter 12

Bissell's Ferry, South Windsor

The ferry began out of necessity. The earliest settlers in Windsor, Connecticut, desired a means of crossing the Farmington and Connecticut Rivers, the latter connecting them with meadows and other resources on the far eastern side of the wide waterway. However, bridges across these waterways were beyond the technological resources of the early settlers.

Recognizing this need, the town of Windsor contracted resident John Bissell, sometime in 1648–1649 to operate a for-profit ferry that would cross the Connecticut River. Charging a fee of 3 pence for a single passenger and 8 pence for each horse or animal transported on his ferryboat (Mooney 2016), Bissell's Ferry was successful from the start and remained in operation until 1925 as one of the longest running ferry services in the United States. Although bridges would eventually be established in the area (today's Bissell Bridge spans the Connecticut River just to the south of the original ferry crossing), Bissell's Ferry managed to retain its local importance and popularity into the 20th century (Fig. 12.1).

All through its history, Bissell's Ferry retained a primitive method of operation. The ferry barge was attached to a submerged cable, the ends of which were secured to trees on opposite banks of the Connecticut River. Using the rudder and leeboard, a plate or board fixed to the side of a flat-bottomed boat that could be lowered into the water to reduce draft to the leeward side, the ferryman would angle the barge so that the river's current would direct the ferry in the desired direction along the submerged cable. For nearly 300 years, this provided the Bissell's Ferry with one of the most historical methods of transport open to travelers.

The original tract of land called 'Windsor' included the east side of the river in present day South Windsor, which was used primarily as 'planting lots' and pasture. However, soon Windsor families would settle 'Bissell's Hill', now known as the village of East Windsor Hill, which would benefit greatly from the success of Bissell's

Fig. 12.1: Postcards dating to the 20th century showing Bissell's Ferry, Windsor, Connecticut (courtesy of the Wood Memorial Library).

monopoly on the river crossing. Of course, Bissell's family had a hand in developing the 'hill', building their own house there in 1658. The ferry was one of the primary transportation routes connecting Hartford/New Haven/New York with Boston and before long the Bissell family was operating a tavern, a stagecoach stop to change horses, three brick houses, and the oldest continuously operating post office in the country (Kremidas 1981). According to the historical marker at the ferry crossing, future President John Adams recorded in his diary: 'Today, I rode through Paradise'.

Originally, John Bissell laid out his ferry crossing north of the confluence of the Scantic and Connecticut Rivers and operated there until 1655 when he moved the ferry's east-side landing to a location on a low terrace just south of the mouth of the Scantic River, in today's South Windsor. Several former structures (houses, tavern, barns, sawmill) related to the early ferry and stage services are believed to have been in a cultivated field that presently borders the tree-lined banks of the Connecticut River. This field is located just south of the junction of the Scantic River with the Connecticut River (Fig. 12.2). A GPR survey was conducted across portions of this field to detect the presence of any remnants to former structures or other buried cultural features associated with Bissell's Landing.

Prior to conducting the GPR survey, a soil map was reviewed to determine the relative suitability of soil conditions within the field for GPR. The field is located within a soil delineation that is labeled '101' (Fig. 12.2). This symbol identifies the dominant soil as Occum fine sandy loam. The very deep (>1.5 m to bedrock), well drained Occum soils formed in alluvial deposits on nearly level floodplains. Each year, many areas of

Occum soils will flood for short periods of time. These soils consist of a loamy solum (A and Bw horizons) overlying a stratified sandy substratum (2C horizons). Occum soils have a low clay content that typically ranges from 2% to 12% in the loamy solum and from 0–5% in the sandy substratum. The solum ranges from about 51 cm to 102 cm (20–40 in) thick. Water moves rapidly through Occum soils and because they commonly lack free water, and have low clay and soluble salt contents, they have relatively low electrical conductivities and are considered well suited to deep, high resolution profiling with GPR.

A SIR-3000 data acquisition system with a 400 MHz antenna were used in this survey. As neither a survey cart or survey wheel was available at the time of this survey, the SIR-3000 was programmed to a time-based rather than distance base mode of operation. As described in earlier chapters, in the time-based mode, the antenna is moved along the surface at a steady speed, and user marks are inserted in the collected data by the radar operator at measured distances that are mark along an antenna guideline. During the post-processing, the time-based radar data were submitted to a distance normalization procedure, which established a constant distance scale between the inserted user marks. All radar data were submitted to standard processing procedures of time-zero correction and background removal, with suitable color table and transform selections. The average velocity of pulse propagation and the depth scale were calculated based on the confirmed depth to a buried reflector that appeared on a radar profile.

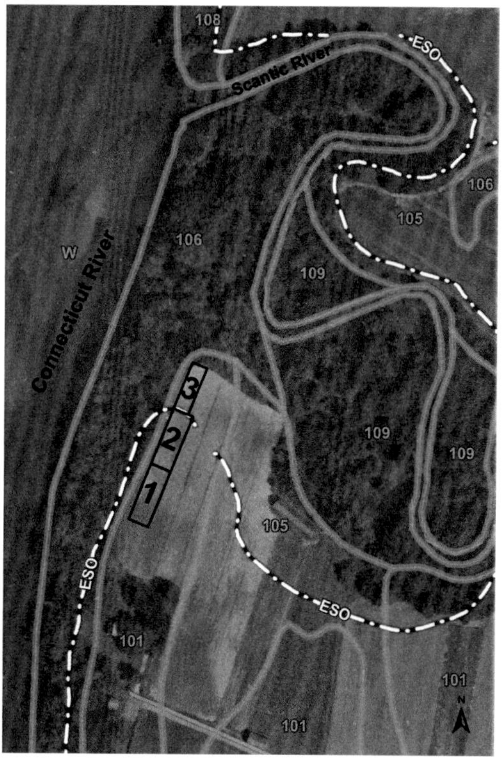

Fig. 12.2: A soil map with the approximate locations of the three GPR grids.

Three grids were established across the north-western edge of the cultivated field. The field is bordered on the west by the tree-line banks of the Connecticut River and on the south by Ferry Lane (Fig. 12.2). Grids were numbered sequentially from south to north (Fig. 12.2, Grids 1, 2, and 3). The dimensions of the grids were: Grid 1, 55 × 25 m; Grid 2, 55 × 23 m; and Grid 3, 45 × 20 m. The grid origin (0, 0 m) was in the south-west corner of each grid. Multiple, parallel radar traverses were conducted along a guideline that was stretch between matching flags on the north and south end lines of each grid (Fig. 12.3). These traverse lines were spaced 50 cm apart. The guideline was marked at intervals of 1 m for distance control.

Fig. 12.3: Conducting the GPR grid survey across a cultivated field adjacent to the Connecticut River (Courtesy of John Spaulding).

Figure 12.4 contains portions of two radar profiles that were collected in Grid 1. The upper profile was collected along X line = 1 m; the lower along X line = 21 m. In each profile, at a depth ranging from about 40–60 cm (16–24 in), a moderately well expressed, linear, layered reflection pattern is evident. This nearly horizontal interface represents the contact of the loamy solum with the underlying sandy substratum of the Occum soil. Below this contact, higher amplitude, more inclined, layered reflection patterns representing the contact of contrasting strata within the predominantly sandy substratum are evident. Because of their higher reflection amplitudes, these strata were presumed to have differing grain size distributions and water contents.

In each radar profile shown in Figure 12.4, black arrows have been inserted to indicate several large, more noticeable, high amplitude, hyperbolic reflection patterns produced by contrasting point anomalies. These more noticeable subsurface anomalies are believed to indicate reflections from larger rock fragments deposited in the sandy alluvial sediments but could also represent buried cultural features. The Occum soils can contain as much as 10% cobbles in its substratum. Cobbles are rounded or partially rounded rock fragments that range from 8–25 cm (3–10 inches) in diameter. Smaller, less obvious reflection hyperbolas within the overlying solum are candidates for buried artifacts (e.g., tools, broken pottery, and glassware) that have been displaced and buried in the soil by mixing processes (pedoturbation) and sedimentation.

On both radar profiles shown in Figure 12.4, vertically elongated, black, dashed rectangles have been inserted to indicate suspected 'multiples' or 'ringing down' patterns from subsurface point reflectors (Conyers 2013). Though the identities of these features were not confirmed and are therefore uncertain, similar reverberating reflection patterns are often attributed to buried metallic features.

The inserted red, dashed lines of a large rectangle in the upper radar profiles (Fig. 12.4) outlines an area of suspected disturbance and possible remnants of a buried structure. This feature consists of a large number of high amplitude reflections at the base of shallower, inwardly dipping reflectors. In sandy soils such as Occum, failure of the soil materials along the sides of trenches and pits is a common occurrence. The concave-upwards reflection pattern that is evident on this radar profile was interpreted by the investigators as a buried former structural feature about 5 m (16 ft) wide.

The lower radar profile in Figure 12.4 typifies the subsurface of Occum soils in the gridded areas that were established within the cultivated field. A close inspection of this radar profile reveals many, small, less obvious, point reflectors in the solum (upper 50 cm of the profile). Do these reflectors represent rock fragments, roots, soil inhomogeneities, or artifacts? Is there an area on this radar profile where the concentration of these point anomalies is sufficient to warrant exploratory excavation by a qualified archaeologist? These were common concerns of the investigators.

The substratum of the Occum soil shown in the lower radar profile in Figure 12.4 reveals the smooth to undulating subsurface topography of several interfaces that separate contrasting layers of sandy alluvium. Portions of these interfaces appear interrupted by breaks, caused by sequential erosion, or by deposited point reflectors (black arrows in Fig. 12.4). Larger, more prominent, anomalous features, many having multiple reflections, have been outlined by dashed, black lines. These anomalous features attracted the attention of investigators but were considered too small or scattered to warrant further attention.

Figure 12.5 contains four depth-slice amplitude images from Grid 1. These depth-slice images are from approximate soil depths of 0 cm, 50 cm, 100 cm,

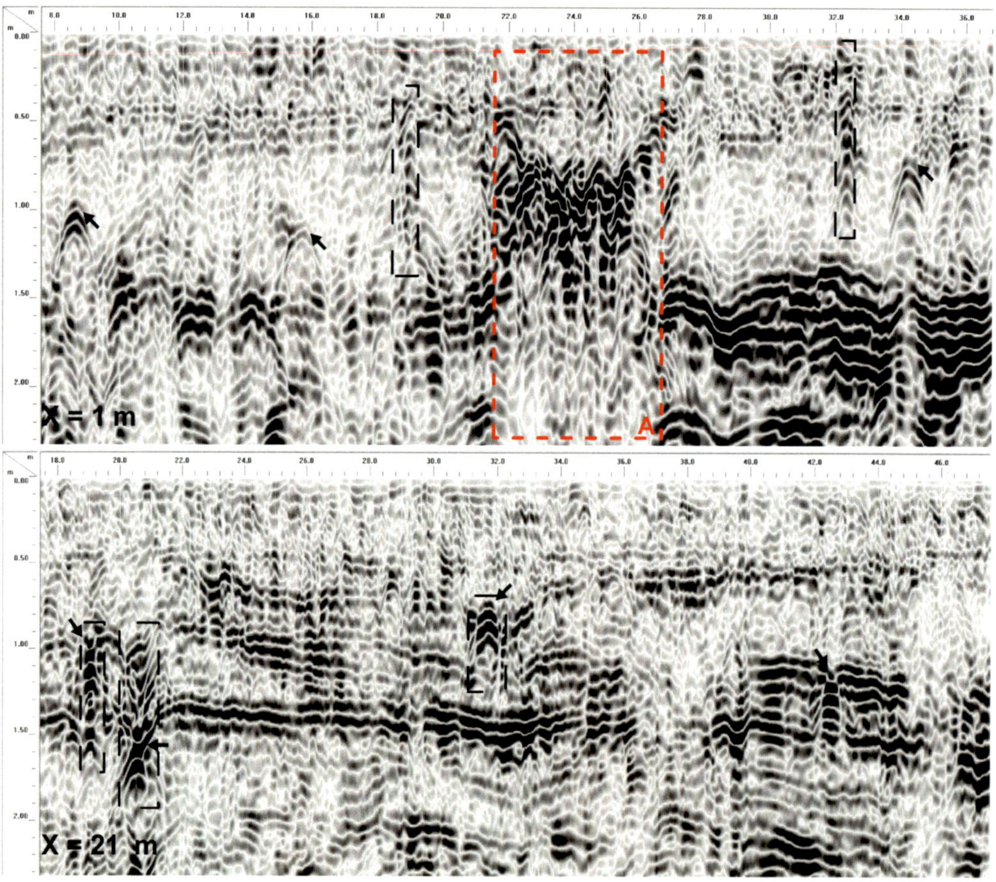

Fig. 12.4: Portions of two radar profiles from Grid 1.

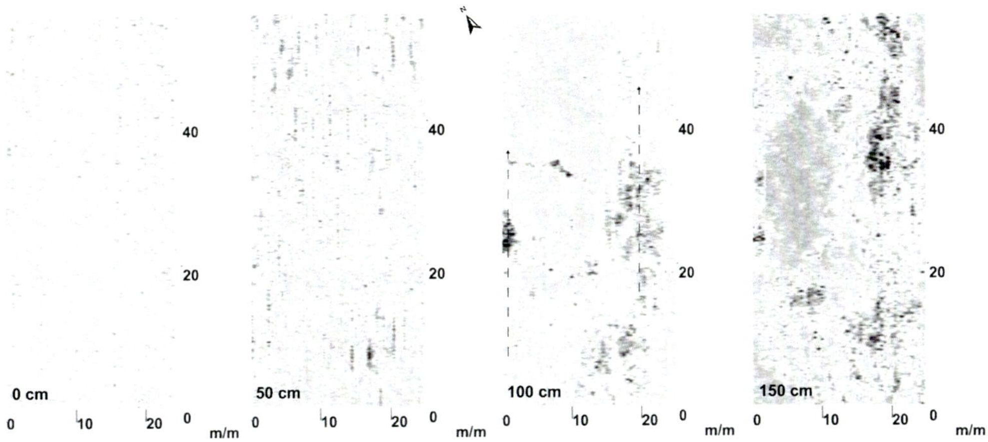

Fig. 12.5: Four depth-slice amplitude images from Grid 1.

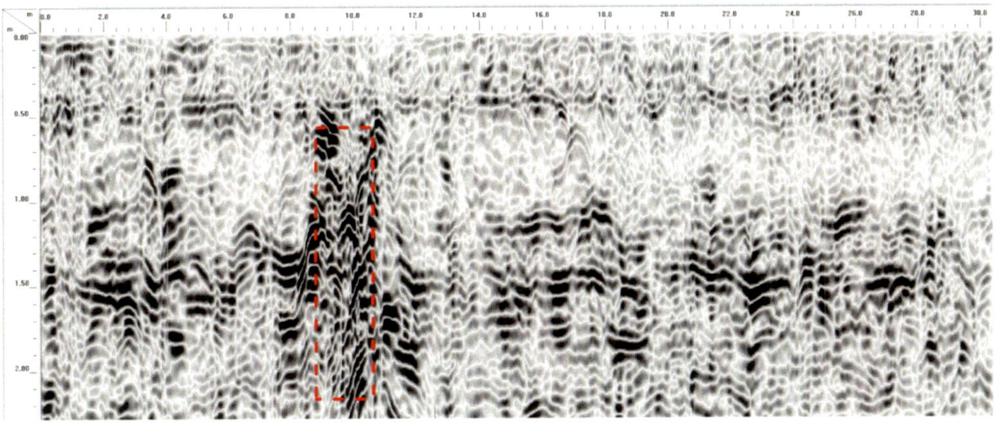

Fig. 12.6: A selected portion of the radar profile from Grid 2, line X = 9.5 m.

and 150 cm. On the 100 cm amplitude depth-slice image the dashed, vertical lines represent the locations of the portions of the two radar profiles shown in Figure 12.4. The 0 cm depth-slice image contains a large number of low amplitude point reflections that are scattered about the grid area with some apparently aligned in vertical rows. Some of these scattered point anomalies could represent artifacts. These point reflectors increase in number and have higher amplitudes on the 50 cm depth-slice image where the vertical alignment of many becomes more apparent. Other than these features, there are no conspicuous or higher amplitude reflection patterns apparent on either of these two depth-slice images.

The 0 cm and 50 cm depth-slice images are unremarkable and provided little useful information to investigators. The vertical patterns of point reflectors are aligned with the direction in which the field is cultivated, and the rows are aligned. Consequently, these reflectors are believed to represent difference in soil compaction attributed to the weight of heavy equipment and tillage implements.

The area of suspected soil disturbance and possible buried structural features noted on the upper radar profile (portion of X line = 1 m) in Figure 12.4 appears as an irregular patch of high amplitude (black) reflections along the Y-axis in the extreme western portion of the 100 cm and 150 cm amplitude depth-slice images. These reflection patterns can be seen along the north-north-easterly trending Y-axis at measured distances ranging from about 21 m to 27 m. This high amplitude reflection pattern appears to extend about 3.5 m into the grid area and decreases in breadth with increasing soil depth. This anomalous feature is believed to extend outside the grid area and into the woodland that adjoins the terrace top break. The location, size, and reflection amplitude of this feature, on both radar profiles and depth-slice amplitude images, were of interest to investigators as it provided the best indication supporting the presence of a possible buried structure in this grid.

The location of the lower radar profile (portion of X line = 21 m) shown in Figure 12.4 appears on the 100 cm and 150 cm depth-slice images within a broad band of noticeably higher amplitude reflections that extend in a general north-north-easterly direction across the gridded area. Overall, within this band, point and linear reflection patterns appear repeatedly but with differing amplitudes. Similar bands span the entire breath of the gridded area. Based on the reflection patterns evident on the radar profiles, these bands were construed to represent the contacts of contrasting layers of alluvium within the substratum of Occum soils.

Figure 12.6 is a portion of the radar profile from line X = 9.5 m of Grid 2. This portion was selected because of the prominence of the anomalous feature enclosed by the red, dashed lines. This anomalous feature appears to cut through the layered reflection patterns within the substratum below a depth of about 50 cm. The layered reflection patterns are believed to represent the boundaries separating contrasting alluvial strata. The feature identified by the red, dashed lines has two noticeable, bordering, vertical reflection patterns. Each vertical pattern consists of multiple point reflectors that suggest a buried stonewall. These two distinct patterns form an area that is about 2 m wide, which includes a central, vertical core of lesser horizontal extent. The core is distinguishable by its comparative lack of reflectors. Based on previous experiences, these patterns suggested to the investigators the presence of a buried well.

Figure 12.7 contains four depth-slice amplitude images of Grid 2. These images are from approximate soil depths of 0 cm, 50 cm, 100 cm, and 150 cm. On the 100 cm amplitude depth-slice image, the dashed vertical line represents the location of the portion of the radar profile shown in Figure 12.6 (line X = 9.5 m). On the 50 cm, 100 cm, and 150 cm depth-slice amplitude images, a square outlined with black, dashed lines indicates the reflections from the prominent subsurface anomaly evident in Figure 12.6.

On the 0 cm and 50 cm depth-slice amplitude images, the grid area lacks any prominent anomaly and consists of a large number of low amplitude point reflections

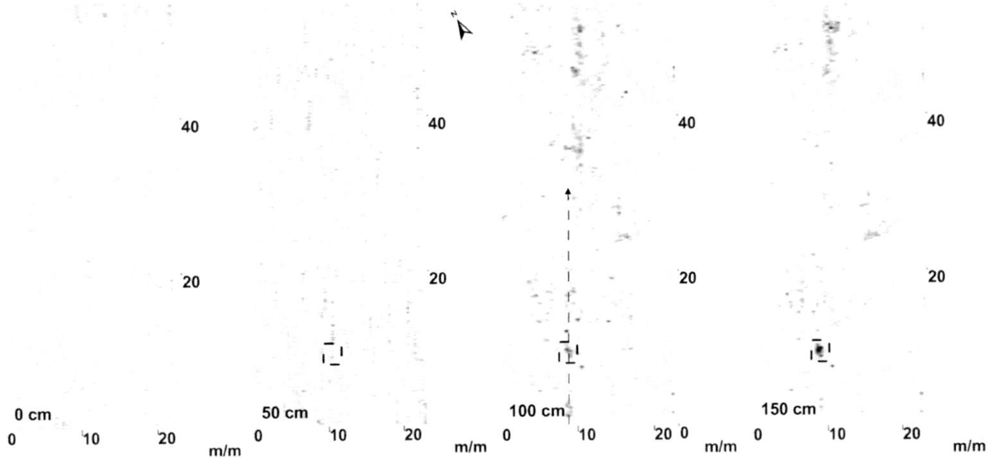

Fig. 12.7: Four depth-slice amplitude images from Grid 2.

that appear to be largely arranged in vertical rows. As previous stated, these point reflectors are believed to represent differences in soil compaction and mark the passage of heavy equipment and tillage implements. However, some may represent cultural debris and artifacts. On the 100 cm and 150 cm images, bands of higher amplitude point reflectors are apparent, especially those in the extreme north-central part of the grid. Here, the bands are aligned in a pattern that corresponds with the orientation of the grid. Following a closer inspection of the radar profiles from this area, these bands were interpreted as representing the contact of contrasting strata and the presence of cobbles in the substratum, rather than remnants of a former built structure. Based on a review of the radar profiles and depth-slice amplitude images from this grid site, the location of the anomalous feature suspected to be a buried well was recorded and recommended for exploratory excavation by a qualified archaeologist, if resources became available.

Grid 3 was the northernmost and smallest grid area surveyed. This grid was also located nearest to the Scantic River (Fig. 12.2). Figure 12.8 is the radar profile from line X = 5.0 m of Grid 3. In Figure 12.8, the radar profile has been divided into two sections (upper and lower profiles) with the middle segment (14.4–30.4 m) repeated on each. This radar profile was selected as it has several distinguishing subsurface anomalies that attracted attention. As on other radar profiles from this site, the contacts separating the solum (A and Bw horizons) from the underlying substratum (2C horizons), and the boundaries separating contrasting layers of sandy alluvium in the substratum are apparent on this profile.

On the radar profile in Figure 12.8, black arrows have been inserted to identify several more conspicuous, high amplitude point reflectors in the substratum. While the identities of these anomalies were not been confirmed, they are believed to represent larger cobbles and boulders. However, the clustering of

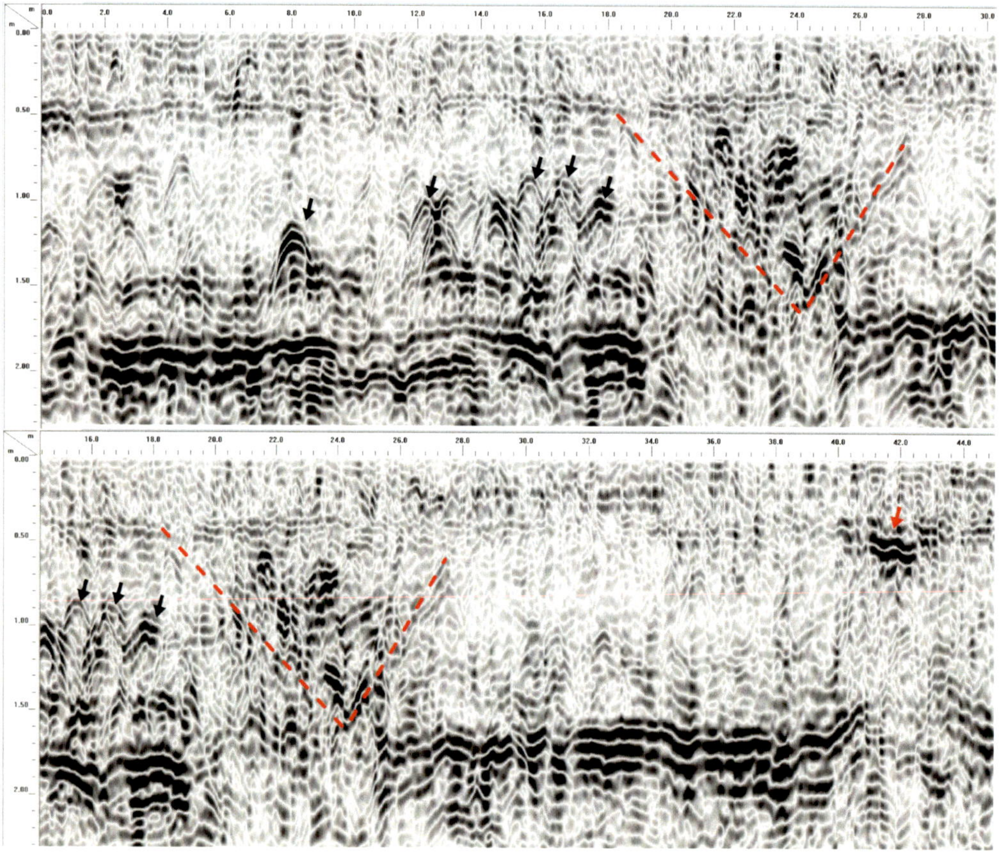

Fig. 12.8: A radar profile from Grid 3, line X = 5 m. The 15–30 m portion of this radar profile is repeated on the two images.

these anomalies between the 12–18 m distance marks was unique in the areas that were surveyed.

The outline of what appears to be a refilled excavation has been identified by two red, dashed lines on the radar profile shown in Figure 12.8. As the substratum of Occum soils is sandy, ranging from loamy fine sands to coarse sands, any unsupported vertical walls of an excavation will slump and possibly form a V-shaped feature such as shown on Figure 12.8. The high amplitude of reflectors within the suspected excavation suggest that this anomalous feature has been refilled with dissimilar materials, perhaps structural remnants of cultural debris.

On the radar record in Figure 12.8, a red arrow has been inserted to identify an anomalous, high amplitude, layered reflection pattern. This horizontally layered pattern occurs between the 40 m and 44 m distance marks and at a depth of about 50 cm on the radar profile. Because of this features uniqueness (e.g., high amplitude, shallow depth, and extent) it attracted the attention of investigators who recorded its location.

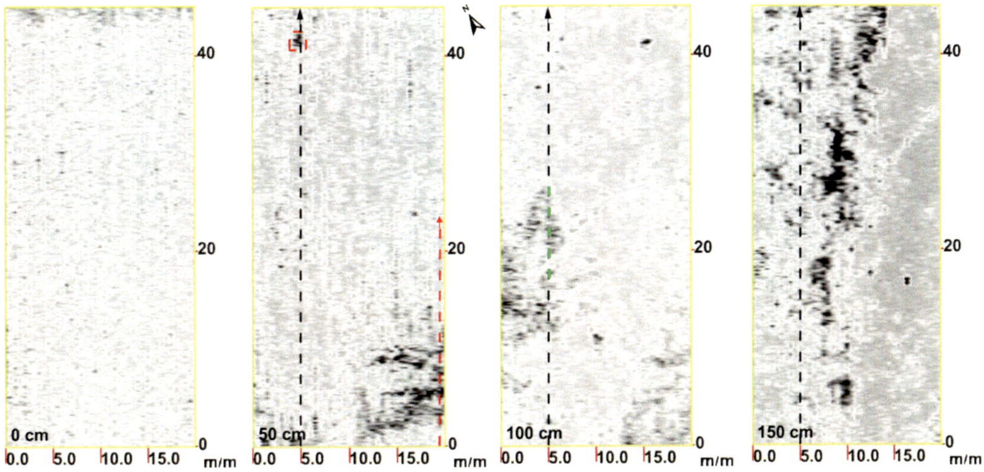

Fig. 12.9. Four depth-slice amplitude images from Grid 3.

Figure 12.9 contains four depth-slice amplitude images of Grid 3. These depth-slice images are from approximate soil depths of 0 cm, 50 cm, 100 cm, and 150 cm. On the 50 cm, 100 cm, and 150 cm images, the black, dashed, vertical line represent the locations of the radar profile shown in Figure 12.8. On the 100 cm depth-slice amplitude image, a green, dashed line has been overlaid on the aforementioned line to indicate the approximate location of the anomalous feature that is suspected to represent a refilled excavation. On the 50 cm image, dashed, red lines have been used to outline the prominent high amplitude, layered reflection pattern that appears on the radar profile (Fig. 12.8) discussed above. Both anomalous features appear as higher amplitude features on these depth-slice images.

On the 50 cm depth-slice image, a conspicuous, anomalous spatial reflection pattern can be seen in the south-east corner of the grid. This pattern has a rectangular appearance with several interior, essentially east–west trending lines of reflections. This anomalous, rectangular-shaped reflection pattern extends into the 100 cm depth-slice image, where it appears more restricted in size and displays lower reflection amplitudes. The internal, linear reflection patterns of this anomalous feature also appear to persist on the 100 cm depth-slice amplitude image. These patterns were believed to represent a former structure with upright stone or masonry walls.

Figure 12.10 is a representative portion of a radar profile from the aforementioned anomalous area. This profile was collected along line X = 19 m. As evident on this radar profile, the uppermost, high amplitude, linear reflection pattern forms an inclined (to the south (left)) layer that merges near the 13 m distance mark into the more weakly expressed contact of the solum with the substratum. The high amplitude of this interface in the first 13 m of the radar profile suggests that the materials are highly contrasting. Two additional, inclined, linear reflection patterns are evident below the more prominent interface. These appear to merge with the upper, more contrasting, layer near the 9 m and 11 m distance marks.

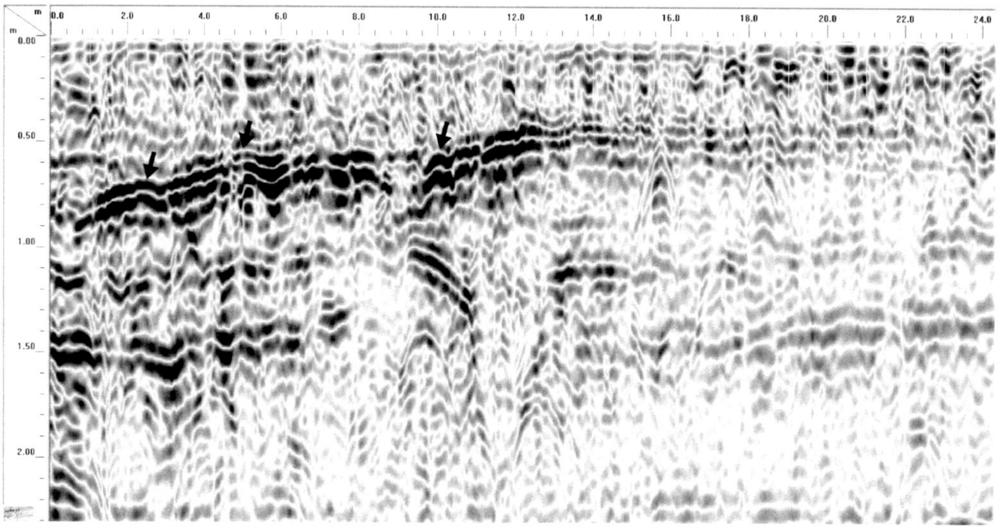

Fig. 12.10: A portion of line X = 19 m from Grid 3.

On the radar profile shown in Figure 12.10, black arrows have been used to indicate three convex-upwards reflection patterns. These reflectors are believed to represent the internal, linear patterns that are evident on the 50 cm and 100 cm depth-slice images shown in Figure 12.9. Each of these appears be underlain by a series of multiple reflections. While not appearing to represent foundation walls, the uniqueness of the linear reflection patterns appearing on depth-slice images and the questionable interpretation of reflection patterns that are seen on radar profiles remains a mystery. The reflection patterns from this area of Grid 3 are believed to represent soil disturbance and possibly remnants of a former structural feature.

Chapter 13

Wightman Burying Ground, Groton

The first Baptist church in Connecticut was organized in the town of Groton when a group (six men and six women) of religious dissenters from the governing Congregational Church called upon the Reverend Valentine Wightman to serve as their pastor. Valentine was an intelligent, educated, enthusiastic, and outspoken, 23 year old young man when summoned to preach to this congregation in 1705. Wightman was the first Baptist preacher in the Connecticut Colony and would serve as the church's pastor until his death in 1747, 42 years later. Daniel Fisk functioned as the church's pastor from 1747 to 1754, followed by Valentine Wightman's son, Timothy, who ministered to the Groton church until his death in 1796. Timothy Wightman's son, John Gano Wightman, would later serve as the pastor of the same church from 1800 to 1841. Thus, a Wightman family member would minister to the Groton Baptist Church for nearly 125 years (Jones 1861, 26–263).

Valentine Wightman's early congregation met at the homes of church members until 1718 (1715 according to some sources; Ancestry Community 2009), when a formal church structure was built (Fig. 13.1). A second church was built in 1790, long after Reverend Valentine's death, but it was abandoned in 1844 when the congregation relocated to Mystic. The abandoned church structure itself was demolished shortly after 1857 (Ancestry Community 2009).

In their rebellion against 'papist' practices, Puritans rejected churchyard burials, as were common in England, as being heretical and idolatrous. In the 17th century, New England townships set aside common land and town greens as burying grounds (Bellantoni 2021, 9). In addition, rural families often developed burying grounds on their private farms. Baptists were often excluded from interring their dead within community graveyards. Hence, Groton's Baptists established their own burying ground in 1710, five years before the construction of the church itself. Given the name 'Wightman' after its founding minister, the burying ground is just under an acre (*c*. 0.5 ha) in size and enclosed by a finished stonewall and having an iron gate entrance (Fig. 13.2).

During the colonial era, places to bury the dead were referred to as 'burying grounds'. These were unplanned spaces where graves could be dug anywhere within the graveyard's boundaries. Hence, there were no established plots or rows, though families were often buried near each other. The first 'planned' cemetery in America was the Grove Street Cemetery, incorporated in 1796, in New Haven, Connecticut, where burial plots were laid out in a grid pattern, mimicking the original town layout of divisions, with paths wide enough for carriages to transverse. This distinction led to a change in nomenclature: before the 19th century, the dead were interred in 'burying grounds'; afterward, they were laid to rest in 'cemeteries', an organized 'sleeping place' (Llewellyn 1998, 24).

Aside from being the resting place of Revolutionary War and Civil War veterans, the Wightman Burying Ground holds the graves of its namesake, Valentine Wightman, his son, Timothy, and grandson, John Gano Wightman, and is the only cemetery in Groton to have an exposed 'wolf stone'. While commonplace in early colonial New England, wolf stones are rarely encountered today. These were rectangular slabs of flat fieldstone(s) placed over burials to prevent wolves from digging into and scattering the remains of the deceased. In 1660, gray wolves were such a problem in the Groton area,

Fig. 13.1: A plaque noting the location of the First Baptist Church of Connecticut at the Wightman Burying Ground in the town of Groton, Connecticut (courtesy of John Spaulding).

Fig. 13.2: The iron gate entrance to the Wightman Burying Ground (courtesy of John Spaulding).

not only by scavenging gravesites but also for killing livestock, that the local farmers offered to give 20 shillings for each wolf that was killed (Absolute Astronomy 2009). This viewpoint of wolves as plunderers and killers contrasts with the perceptions of local Native Americans. Mohegan/Pequot tribes of the area held a more positive and reverent point of view toward wolves (Moses 2022), thus, having contrasting cultural-ecological beliefs with the colonists that they shared the countryside with. Regardless of Native perspectives, Colonial Connecticut celebrated the news of the killing of the last wolf by Israel Putnam in Putnam in 1742. With the elimination of the last grey wolf, wolf stones were no longer necessary to protect the bodies and many were uprooted from the graves to be used as capstones for bordering stonewalls, or simply discarded. While wolf stones are rarely found exposed in Connecticut Cemeteries, some could still be preserved in the ground beneath a very shallow covering of grasses and organic and mineral soil materials (Marteka 2010).

In 1716, John Burrows Sr was buried in the Wightman Burying Ground in Groton, with his grave covered by a large flat wolf stone extending between a legibly inscribed tombstone and an initialed footstone. The wolf stone remains intact and is still visible above ground (Fig. 13.3). This being the only wolf stone exposed in the graveyard, and one of the most notable in the state of Connecticut, the Groton historical community requested a GPR survey to ascertain whether other wolf stones are present but no longer visible due to being covered over time by a thin mantle composed of invading grasses and earthen materials.

Fig. 13.3: John Burrows Sr's (1642–1716) grave in the Wightman Burying Ground is covered with a large flat stone known as a 'wolf stone' to keep the grave from being dug up by animals (courtesy of John Spaulding).

Fig. 13.4: The Wightman Burying Ground (outlined with white, dashed line) is in an area of dominantly shallow and moderately deep soils that are underlain by tabular gneiss bedrock.

The Wightman Burying Ground is near the site of the first Baptist church that was established in Connecticut. The cemetery is located on the west side of Cold Spring Road just north of the road's junction with Godfrey and Yetter roads in Groton, Connecticut. A soil survey map of the area reveals that the Wightman Cemetery (white dashed rectangle on Fig. 13.4) is located within a soil delineation labeled '75C'. This symbol identifies the soil map unit as Hollis–Chatfield–Rock Outcrop complex, on 3–15% slopes. The shallow (<50 cm to bedrock), somewhat excessively drained Hollis and the moderately deep (50–100 cm to bedrock), well drained Chatfield soils formed in glacial till. These soils have rock fragment contents that can range from 5% to 50% by volume. The underlying bedrock is the variably lineated and foliated Hope Valley Alaskite Gneiss of Proterozoic age. Because the Hollis and Chatfield soils commonly lack free water and have low clay, soluble salt contents and electrical conductivities, they are considered well suited to deep, high resolution profiling with GPR. However, if the soils at this site have been properly identified and mapped, their relatively shallow depths to hard bedrock would offer limited potentials for gravesites.

Due to the short available time, only a cursory GPR survey was possible. Several random GPR traverses were completed near older (pre-1750s) gravestones, and across open areas of the burying ground that had no records of burials and were free of gravestones. This survey was completed using a SIR-3000 data acquisition system with a 400 MHz antenna. Neither a distance-measuring survey cart nor survey wheel was used in this survey. Radar data was simply collected in a time mode as the 400 MHz antenna was moved at a slow, but steady, walking pace along a guideline that was stretched across an open area of interest (Fig. 13.5). During data collection, no distance marks were inserted on the radar file. Consequently, the horizontal scale on all collected radar profiles would remain as a time rather than distance scale. However, whenever the antenna passed before a gravestone, a user mark was impressed on the radar file to identify its location.

Fig. 13.5: Conducting the GPR survey across an open area of the Wightman Burying Ground (courtesy of John Spaulding).

During post-processing, the collected radar data were submitted to standard processing procedures of time-zero correction, with suitable color table and transform selections. The average velocity of pulse propagation and the depth scale were estimated by hyperbola matching.

Random GPR traverses were conducted across different portions of the burying ground to locate unmarked graves and additional wolf stones. A preliminary traverse was conducted across the site of John Burrows Sr's grave, which has the exposed wolf stone. Figure 13.6 is the radar profile from this traverse. The vertical scale along the left-hand margin is a depth scale (in meters). The horizontal scale was in nanoseconds (time scale) and has been omitted from this image.

The radar profile in Figure 13.6 contains an exceedingly large number of widely dispersed and chaotically arranged reflectors of varying amplitudes. On this complicated radar profile, recognizable and meaningful spatial patterns are difficult to distinguish. The high level of undesired background noise obscures the recognition of graves. The white arrow identifies the reflection pattern produced by the John Burrows Sr wolf stone. This conspicuous, short, flat-lying, high amplitude, layered reflection pattern was used to help guide the identification of other potential wolf stones in the burying ground. Except for the Burrows Sr wolf stone, user marks (each numbered to the right of the short, dashed vertical lines) have been inserted on the radar profile as the antenna was drawn passed sets of gravestones (headstone and footstone). The white, dashed rectangles inserted on this profile outline what are perceived to be the edges of grave shafts. Though the difference is subtle and perhaps too imaginative, the radar reflections within these rectangles appear to be dissimilar from adjacent sections and have inwardly slumping patterns that suggest the settling of refilled soil materials in a grave shaft. As these patterns occur near gravestones, presumptions of grave sites were unavoidable. The light, blue arrow points to high amplitude, linear reflection patterns that are similar to the known and identified (with white arrow) wolf stone. These wolf stone-like reflection patterns appear within

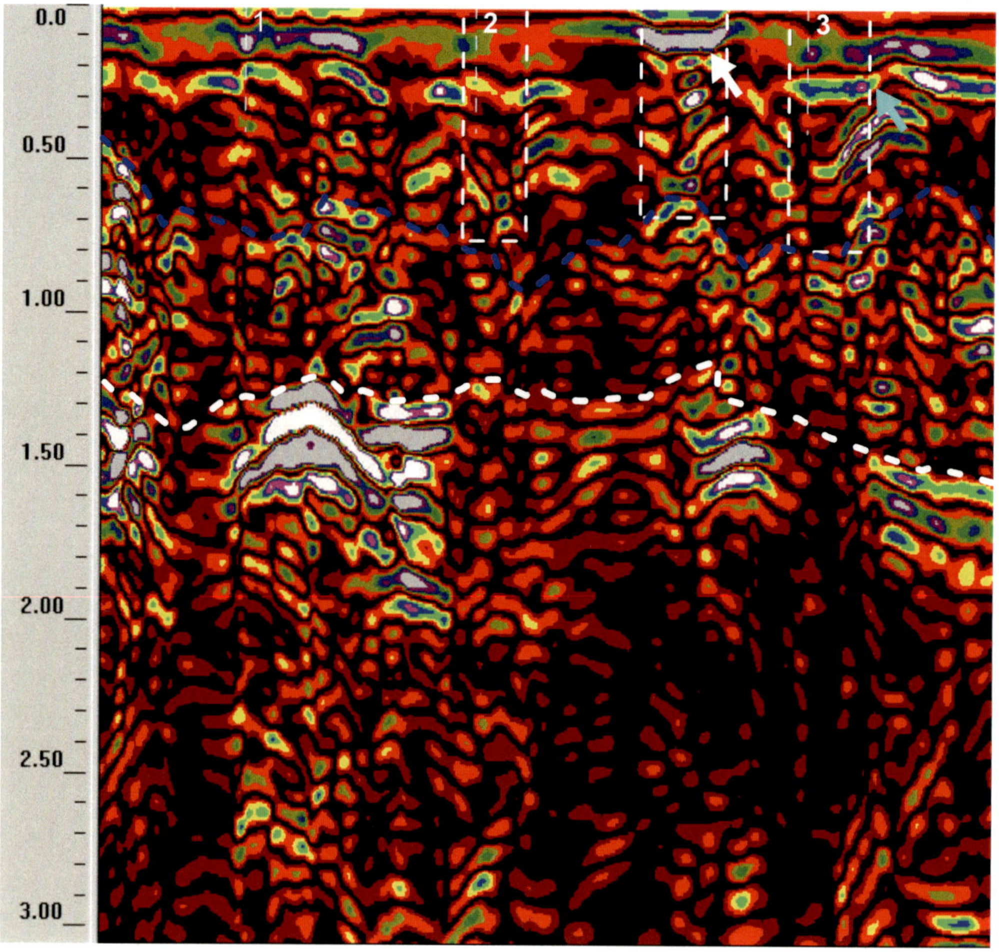

Fig. 13.6: A radar profile containing the reflection pattern produced by the John Burrow Sr wolf stone and adjoining marked grave sites.

soil depths of about 25 cm (10 in). These reflection anomalies could not be excavated and identified as they occurred at commemorated gravesites.

Two wavy, dashed, horizontal lines have been inserted on the radar profile in Figure 13.6 to subdivide the underlying stratigraphy and lithology. The upper, blue, dashed line separates what is believed to be the soil and glacial till from highly fractured and frost-heaved bedrock. If this interpretation is correct, the depth to bedrock in this area of the cemetery would be between soil depths of 50–100 cm (20–39 in). If this is the actual depth to bedrock, the reflections from the interpreted graves would be exceptionally shallow and the soils would be the moderately deep Chatfield. The underlying Hope Valley Alaskite Gneiss is known to break into coarse fragments and thick tabular slabs. Extreme fracturing of this rock would be caused by mechanical frost weathering and occur presumably along joints in the rock. It is possible that frost wedging, which largely occurred during glaciation and in past periglacial environments, fragmented the rock in well-jointed portions.

Fig. 13.7: Two additional wolf stones found in the Wightman Burying Ground (courtesy of John Spaulding).

The lower, white line is used to separate the more fractured from the thicker and more tabular gneiss. Several high amplitude reflection (white and gray) patterns occur along this lower line. While the features causing these high amplitude reflections are unknown, they may represent short bands and lenses of varying mineral assemblages embedded in the gneiss. Along the extreme left-hand edge of this radar profile, a vertical pattern consisting of multiple, high-amplitude point reflectors is apparent. While the full horizontal extent of this feature(s) was not included in this radar traverse, its uniqueness attracted the attention of archaeologists. Because this feature occurred near a marked grave site it was not investigated.

Further radar traverses were conducted across several open areas within the burying ground that contain no known grave sites or visible grave markers. In all but one radar traverse, no reflection patterns were apparent that suggested an unmarked grave or wolf stone. However, along one traverse, two closely spaced, short, flat-lying, high amplitude linear reflection patterns were observed at a very shallow depth. These patterns were immediately associated with wolf stones. As the Connecticut State Archaeologist and volunteers from the Friends of the Office of State Archaeology were present, the soil overburden was carefully removed revealing the presence of two closely spaced wolf stones (Fig. 13.7). Though near to gravestones, these wolf stones are separate and not associated with these grave markers. Other than these two confirmed wolf stones, the GPR revealed no clear evidence that would support the presence of unmarked graves in the open areas that were traversed in the Wightman Burying Ground. However, as the radar profiles contained a high level of background noise, and older burial sites could be easily missed when interpreting radar profiles, caution should still be used if excavations are planned in these open areas.

Chapter 14

Conclusions

In each of the studies discussed in this book, the Connecticut State Archaeologist was approached by local historians, historical societies, non-profit groups, and/or cemetery superintendents for assistance in resolving an issue that had arisen at a site of cultural interest in Connecticut. After discussing the historical background knowledge and concerns with these individuals, the Connecticut State Archaeologist recommended a ground-penetrating radar (GPR) investigation of each site. Because of the limited availability of GPR services, each survey had to be completed in one day. Therefore, the size of the survey area was restricted and had to be well defined, based on the knowledge of the participants.

Based on established information and/or observations, small grids were established at nine of the twelve historical sites discussed. Line or random walk surveys were conducted at the other three sites. Grid surveys are considered the most efficient method to comprehensively chart the subsurface and detect buried historical features (Conyers and Goodman 1997). A dense array of grid lines is recommended to detect and resolve most subsurface features and to reduce spatially aliasing (Grasmueck and Green 1996). We have used grid line spacings of 10 cm and 25 cm (4–10 in) for the investigation of some gravesites. However, because of considerations for the size of the sites and the limited time and resources that were available, a grid line spacing of 50 cm was used and considered adequate for nine of the ten grid sites. For the investigation of the runway at Bradley International Airport (Chapter 9), where survey time was restricted to several hours and the feature of interest was considered sizable, a grid line interval of 1 m (3.3 ft) was used. Line or random walk surveys were conducted to quickly assess the dimensions of a buried crypt in the North Burying Ground in Danbury (Chapter 5), to locate remnants of a former stockade wall in the heavily forested Barkhamsted Cemetery (Chapter 6), and to search for hidden wolf stones in the Wightman Burying Ground in Groton (Chapter 13).

For each survey, a state-of-the-art radar system was used. Early surveys were conducted with a SIR-3000 data acquisition system; later surveys were conducted with a SIR-4000 data acquisition system. As survey wheels and carts became available, they were used. Antennas that operated at center frequencies of 80, 120, 200, 300, 400, 500, and 900 MHz were available for each investigation. However, based on previous experiences searching for buried historical artifacts in the soils of Connecticut, the 400 MHz antenna is considered to provide the best balance of required resolution and observation depth (0–1.5 m; 0–4.9 ft).

All collected radar data was submitted to standard processing procedures using an advanced GPR processing software that was well suited to our needs. The selected data processing procedures used in our investigations were familiar and had produced suitable results in previous studies.

An understanding of the soils and their respective physical and chemical properties at an investigation site is vital to the effective use of GPR and the interpretation of results. Most soils in Connecticut are considered generally well suited to GPR as they allow deep (1.5 m) penetration with high resolution antennas (>350 MHz). However, some soils afford more restricted penetration depths especially for higher resolution antennas. Each author has over 20 years of experience using GPR for archaeological investigations in Connecticut. They have worked in most soils that occur in the state and know how these soils should appear on radar profiles. Knowledge of soil properties and likely soil inclusions (e.g., rock fragments, tree roots, animal burrows, modern cultural features, disturbance signatures or debris, segmented horizons, and stratigraphic layers) benefits the interpretation of radar imagery.

Ground-penetrating radar provides continuous spatial imaging of the subsurface along traverse lines. This geophysical technique can produce comprehensive subsurface information about a site, detect buried historical features, and help minimize the number of unsuccessful exploratory pits. It offers a rapid, cost-effective, and non-destructive means to locate and, sometimes, identify buried artifacts. However, the use of GPR complements, but does not replace, the need for conventional archaeological methodologies.

Ground-penetrating radar detects, but does not identify, subsurface features. The successful interpretation of GPR imagery depends upon the experience of the operator, the properties of the buried artifact or structure, the complexity of soil or geologic materials, the quantity and quality of independent knowledge and observational data, and the system and antennas used. The levels of confidence that can be attached to interpretations of GPR data will depend upon these factors.

The interpretation of buried artifacts and structural features on radar profiles and depth-slice amplitude imagery is challenging and often ambiguous if undertaken without reliance on historical information to guide and ground-truth excavations to confirmed interpretations. The sites showcased here deliberately demonstrate not only the potential and efficacy of GPR but also the ambiguities and uncertainties of survey results. Ground-truth excavations were imaginable and achieved at only four of the twelve sites: the investigation of the hidden tomb at the North Burying

Ground in Danbury, the search for the former palisade wall in Windsor, the search for remnants of past outbuildings at the Elijah Welles House in Newington, and the search for hidden wolf stones in the Wightman Burying Ground in Groton.

At the Robinson Burying Grounds in Stonington (Chapter 2), GPR profiles and depth-slice amplitude imagery revealed the location of a large V-shaped subsurface reflection anomaly. While the actual cause(s) for this feature is unknown, it was attributed to a refilled crater that was produce by an exploding British cannon ball; and interpretation that supported the historical legend.

Twenty Frenchmen were reportedly buried during the Revolutionary War beneath the entryway to the Old Norwich Burying Ground in Norwichtown (Chapter 3). A group of closely spaced hyperbolas appearing on radar profiles and two conspicuous sets of linear reflection patterns on depth-slice amplitude images suggested buried 'grave-like' features along a portion of the entryway. While the location for these anomalies conforms to historical documents, the high amplitudes of these reflection hyperbolas and spatial patterns were not expected for 250 year old burials, which should be highly decomposed and indistinct on radar imagery.

In many cemeteries, memories fade, historical records are lost or misplaced, and grave markers are lost or relocated over time. The presumed location for the unmarked grave of Jeff Liberty and his wife had been commemorated by a wooden stake and an American flag at the Old Judea Cemetery in Washington (Chapter 4). Could GPR provide any evidence supporting this conclusion? Reflection hyperbolas appearing on several radar profiles collected in the area surrounding the presumed grave site suggested possible remnants from unmarked grave sites. One of these anomalous reflection hyperbolas occurred close to the presumed grave site for Jeff Liberty and his wife. The coincidence of this reflection anomaly with the presumed location of the unmarked grave site was accepted as sufficient evidence for the positioning of a monument to Jeff Liberty by the Connecticut Sons of the American Revolution.

Curiosity prompted a preliminary archaeological excavation along the base of an exposed concrete slab within the North Burying Ground in Danbury. The reasons for the presence of this slab were unknown. Excavation carried out by the State Archaeologist revealed a marble door to a concealed tomb. Knowledge of this tomb's existence prompted several random walk GPR traverses across the top of this feature to non-invasively determine its dimensions and depth (Chapter 5). The measurements obtain from this brief GPR survey were used to guide an endoscopic inspection of the vault's interior.

Several random walk radar GPR traverses were used to help identify the location a former wooden stockade fence that had been erected in the 1930s by the Civilian Conservation Corps (CCC) around the Lighthouse Village Cemetery in Barkhamsted (Chapter 6). Anomalous reflection patterns that appeared on radar profiles supported visual observations made at the site and helped to verify the location of a corner of the former stockade fence. Additional GPR traverses prompted thoughts concerning the presence and conditions of 'grave-like' anomalies within the cemetery.

Ground-penetrating radar was used to investigate the former waterfront of the 19th century village of Pettipaug and the site of a historic battle in Essex (Chapter 7). The former waterfront has been buried by humanly-transported fill materials and covered by pavement. Results from the GPR survey revealed indications of previous archaeological excavations and a buried historic bulkhead wharf. The GPR interpretations may be used as supporting evidence to help place this site on the National Register of Historic Places.

The reason for many rectangular-shaped, shallow depressions in an unused portion of the Old Farm Cemetery in Middletown was non-intrusively explored with GPR (Chapter 8). Multiple, contrasting, columnar-shaped patterns on radar profiles, and east–west extended 'grave-like' patterns on depth-slice amplitude images were observed on the collected radar imagery. These anomalous patterns were attributed to unmarked graves from the 1918 flu pandemic. Because of the sensitivity of this site, no ground-truth excavations were possible. However, based on the GPR imagery and site observations, posts were erected around the grid site to commemorate and preserve the unmarked graves.

Ground-penetrating radar was used on a runway at the Bradley International Airport to confirm the site where Lt Eugene Bradley crashed his plane in 1941 (Chapter 9). Earlier archaeological investigations at several potential sites had produced negative findings. However, the most probable location of the crash was determined to be underneath a runway and therefore inaccessible to standard archaeological methods, but briefly available to GPR. Interpretations of GPR imagery collected over the runway revealed what appeared to be a large, extended, refilled trench-like subsurface feature but no anomaly that matched the expected shape and dimensions of a plane crash.

During the Pequot War (1636–1638) the settlement at Dorchester (Windsor) erected a picket palisade to surround their houses. A GPR investigation was carried out to detect remnants of this former wooden palisade and other former structures (Chapter 10). The presence of scattering bodies (large tree roots, rocks, animal burrows, and soil inhomogeneities) in the soil confounded GPR interpretations. However, based on radar interpretations, two test pits were dug by archaeologists. One excavation contained two closely spaced cable lines beneath what was projected to be the location of the former picket palisade. The other excavation revealed a mantle of humanly-transported and altered materials that contained artifacts dating back to the 17th and 18th centuries.

A GPR survey was conducted in the backyard of the Elijah Wells' house in Newington to identify possible buried historical features (Chapter 11). Radar profiles revealed reflections from what appeared to be scattered cultural debris (e.g., bricks, pipes, tools, and shards of glass and pottery) and buried foundations. Near an excavation that revealed a subsurface brickwork foundation, an anomalous reflection pattern was inferred to represent the extension of this buried feature. In addition, depth-slice amplitude imagery revealed two parallel, linear reflectors, spaced about 1 m apart, extending across the grid. The shallow depth and appearance of these reflectors suggested the boundaries of a former walkway.

Portions of a cultivated field in Windsor were surveyed with GPR to detect remnants of former structures (houses, tavern, barn, sawmill) related to the historical Bissell Ferry (Chapter 12). Conspicuous reflection patterns that appeared on radar profiles and depth-slice images were, based on previous experiences, attributed to former buildings, a well, and a refilled excavation. No archaeological excavations could be completed to confirm these interpretations.

Ground-penetrating radar was used to locate buried wolf stones in the Wightman Cemetery in Groton (Chapter 13). Analyses of the radar profiles disclosed reflections that appeared to represent additional wolf stones in the cemetery. A push probe was used to confirm the presence and a shallow excavation revealed the identity of two closely spaced wolf stones. No other indications of reflection anomalies from unmarked burials in vacant areas of the cemetery were noticed.

References

Absolute Astronomy. 2009. http://www.absoluteastronomy.com/topics/Groton,_Connecticut.

Acari, R. D. and Birden, H. 1997. *The 1918 Influenza Epidemic in Connecticut*, Vol. 38. New Haven, CT, Association for the Study of Connecticut History.

Ancestry Community. 2009. http://freepages.genealogy.rootsweb.ancestry.com/~wightman/Valentine1681.htm

Banner, J. M. 1970. *To the Hartford Convention: the Federalists and the origins of party politics in Massachusetts, 1789–1815*, New York, Knopf.

Barry, J. M. 2004. *The Great Influenza: The Epic Story of the Deadliest Plague in History*. New York, Penguin Books.

Baxter, E. S. 1971. *The Centennial History of Newington*. Hartford CT, Lucy Robbins Welles Library

Becker, A. M. 2004. Smallpox in Washington's army: strategic implications of the disease during the American Revolution. *The Journal of Military History* 68(2), 381–430.

Bell, M. 1985. *The Faces of Connecticut: people, geology, and the land*. Hartford CT, State Geological and Natural History Survey of Connecticut Bulletin 110.

Bellantoni, N. 2021. *And So The Tomb Remained: exploring archaeology and forensic science within Connecticut's historical family mausolea*. Oxford, Oxbow Books.

Bevan, B. W. 1991. The search for graves. *Geophysics* 56 (9), 1310–19.

Cassidy, N. J. 2009. Electrical and magnetic properties of rocks, soils, and fluids. In: Jol, H. M. (ed.), *Ground Penetrating Radar: theory and applications*, 41–72. Amsterdam, Elsevier.

Caulkins, F. M. 1845. *History of Norwich, Connecticut from its Settlement in 1660, to January 1845*. Norwich CT, Case, Tiffany and Burnham, Hartford, Connecticut.

Connecticut Environmental Conditions Online. 2010. https://cteco.uconn.edu/resource/CT ECO_Resource_Guide_Soils_Drainage.pdf

Connecticut History nd. https://connecticuthistory.org/outcasts-build-their-own-village-in-18th-century-barkhamsted/

Conyers, L. B. 2011. Discovery, mapping, and interpretation of buried cultural resources non-invasively with ground-penetrating radar. *Journal of Geophysics and Engineering* 8, S13–S22.

Conyers, L. B. 2013. *Ground-Penetrating Radar for Archaeology* (3rd edn). Walnut Creek, CA, AltaMira Press.

Conyers, L. B. and Goodman, D. 1997. *Ground-penetrating Radar: an introduction for archaeologists*. Walnut Creek CA, AltaMira Press.

Cregeau, D. 2020. Ten Patriot Soldier gravesites. *Journal of the American Revolution* 29 October. https://allthingsliberty.com/2020/10/ten-patriot-soldier-gravesites/

Crosby, A. 2003. *America's Forgotten Pandemic: The Influenza of 1918*. Cambridge, Cambridge University Press.

CT DEEP and USDA NRCS. 2022. *Soil Catenas of Connecticut*. Tolland CT: Connecticut Geological Survey, Office of Information Management, Connecticut Department of Energy and Environmental Protection and USDA Natural Resources Conservation Service.

Cummins, T., Lewis, H., Ní Lionáin, C. and Davis, S. 2018. Soils and archaeology. In: Creamer, R. and O'Sullivan, L. (eds), *The Soils of Ireland*. 267–80. Cham, Springer World Soils. https://doi.org/10.1007/978-3-319-71189-8_19

Daniels, D. J. 2004. *Ground Penetrating Radar* (2nd edn). London, Institute of Electrical Engineers.

Day, S. 2020. A look back in Middletown provides insight into today's pandemic. *The Middletown Press* 24 August. https://www.middletownpress.com/middletown/article/A-look-back-in-Middletown-provides-insight-into-15506526.php

de Kay, J. T. 1990. *The Battle of Stonington: Torpedoes, Submarines, and Rockets in the War of 1812.* Annapolis ML, United States Naval Institute.

Doolittle, J. A. and Bellantoni, N. F. 2010. The search for graves with ground-penetrating radar in Connecticut. *Journal of Archaeological Science* 37 (5), 941–9.

Doolittle, J. A., Minzenmayer, F. E., Waltman, S. W., Benham, E. C., Tuttle, J. W. and Peaslee, S. 2007. Ground-penetrating radar soil suitability map of the conterminous United States. *Geoderma* 141 (3/4), 416–21.

Drury, D. 2020. The Spanish Influenza Pandemic of 1918, https://connecticuthistory.org/the-spanish-influenza-pandemic-of-1918/.

Ellis, J. H. 2009. *A Ruinous and Unhappy War: New England and the war of 1812.* New York, Algora.

Feder, K. L. 1994. *A Village of Outcasts: historical archaeology and documentary research at the Lighthouse Site.* Mountain View, CA, Mayfield.

Feder, K. 2009. *Barkhamsted Lighthouse. Barkhamsted Lighthouse Archaeological Preserve, Barkhamsted, Connecticut.* https://connecticuthistory.org/outcasts-build-their-own-village-in-18th-century-barkhamsted/

Fiedler, S., Illich, B., Berger, J. and Graw, M. 2009. The effectiveness of ground-penetrating radar surveys in the location of unmarked burial sites in modern cemeteries. *Journal of Applied Geophysics* 68 (3), 380–5.

Grasmueck, M. and Green, A. G. 1996. 3-D georadar mapping: looking into the subsurface. *Environmental and Engineering Geoscience* 2 (2), 195–220.

Greenburg, L. 2006. Reach for the Channel: some documentary and archaeological evidence of extending the Alexandria's waterfront. *The Alexandria Chronicle* Spring, 1–13.

Hale, C.R. 1935. *Charles R. Hale Collection of Connecticut Cemetery Inscriptions.* Connecticut State Library, Hartford, CT.

Haynes, W. 1949. *Stonington Chronology: being a year-by-year record of the American way of life in a Connecticut town.* Stonington CT: Pequot Press.

Howard, D. 1935. *A New History of Old Windsor, Connecticut.* Windsor Lock, CT, The Journal Press.

Huntington, J. 1923. Letter to Jabez Huntington, 25 October 1778. *Huntington papers, Part I, Correspondence of Col. Joshua Huntington (and other members of the Huntington Family*, 31. Hartford, CT, Collections of the Connecticut Historical Society 20.

Jones, Rev. H. 1861. Early Baptists in Connecticut. In: Bacon, L., Dutton, S. W. S. and Robinson, E. W. (eds), *Contributions to the Ecclesiastical History of Connecticut*, 262–3. New Haven CT, William L. Kingsley.

Junck, M.B. and Jol, H. M. 2000. Three-dimensional investigation of geomorphic environments using ground penetrating radar. In: Noon, D. (ed.), *Proceedings of the Eight International Conference on Ground-Penetrating Radar. May 23 to 26, 2000*, 314–18. Gold Coast, Queensland, University of Queensland.

Kibblewhite, M., Toth, G. and Hermann, T. 2015. Predicting the preservation of cultural artefacts and buried materials in soils. *Science of the Total Environment* 529, 249–63.

Kremidas, L. J. 1981. *The History of South Windsor Connecticut: Settlement to Incorporation 1634–1845.* http//www.southwindsor-ct.gov.

Leach, P. 2021. *A Theory Primer and Field Guide for Archaeological, Cemetery, and Forensic Surveys with Ground Penetrating Radar.* Nashua NH, Geophysical Survey Systems, Inc, MN10-376 Rev A.

Llewellyn, J. F. 1998. *A Cemetery Should BE Forever: the challenge to managers and directors.* Glendale, CA, Tropico Press.

Lord, B. 1778 [1783]. *The Aged Minister's Solemn Appeal to God, and Serious Address to his People. Being the Substance of the Tenth and Eleventh Annual Discourse, after the Half-century at Norwich, November 21, 1778, with a Dedicatory Preface. Benjamin Lord, A.M. Senior Pastor of the First Church There.* Norwich CT, Printed by John Trumbull 1783.

Marteka, P. 2010. State Archaeologist asked to find 'wolf stones' in church cemetery *Hartford Courant* 10 November.

Middletown Death Records 1921. *Middletown Death Records* 31. New Haven, CT, Tuttle, Morehouse, & Taylor.

Miller, P. S. 1996. Disturbances in the soil: finding buried bodies and other evidence using ground penetrating radar. *Journal of Forensic Science* 41, 648–52.

Mills, L. S. 1952. *The legend of Barkhamsted Light House: A Tale From the Litchfield Hills of Connecticut.* Barkhamsted, CT, Lewis S. Mills.

Mooney, J. F. 2016. The lost years of Bissell's Ferry. *Windsor Historical Society Chronicles* 34, 4.

Moore, G. H. 1862. *Historical Notes on the Employment of Negroes in the American Army of the Revolution.* New York, Charles T. Evans.

Moses, K. 2022. *Indians, Wolves, and Colonists: How Colonial Power Left an Incomplete Framework for Wolf Narratives in the Native Northeast.* Hartford, CT, The Trinity Papers, Trinity College Digital Repository. https://digitalrepository.trincoll.edu/trinitypapers/107.

NEAM. 1998. *Bradley Field: the First 25 Years.* East Granby, CT, New England Air Museum.

Palmer, H. R. 1913. *Stonington by the Sea.* Stonington, CT, Palmer Press.

Palshaw, T. 2008. *Research project: relocate the crash site of 2LT Eugene M. Bradley, August 21, 1941.* East Granby CT, New England Air Museum.

Palshaw, T. C. 2018. The search for historic truth; the search for Lt. Eugene M. Bradley's Crash Site. *American Aviation Historical Society Journal*, 113–22.

Plummer, D. 2020. Norwich in a Nutshell: The mystery of the French soldiers. *The Day.* https://www.theday.com/article/20201001/NWS01/201009990

Roberts, J. 2020. *The British Raid on Essex; the forgotten battle of the war of 1812.* Guilford, CT, Lyons Press.

Savas, S. 2004. *The War That Came Home: The Individuals That Personalized the 1918 Influenza Epidemic in Middletown, Connecticut.* Special Collections & Archives, Wesleyan University, Student Papers.

Skehan, J. W. 2008. *Roadside Geology of Connecticut and Rhode Island.* Misoula MO, Mountain Press.

Soil Survey Staff. 2022. *Natural Resources Conservation Service, United States Department of Agriculture. Web Soil Survey.* http://websoilsurvey.sc.egov.usda.gov/.

Starr, B. P. 1879. *A History of the Starr Family of New England, From the Ancestor, Dr. Comfort Starr, of Ashford, County of Kent, England, Who Emigrated to Boston, Mass., in 1636.* Hartford, CT, Case, Lockwood & Brainerd.

Steenburg, N. 2012. Attack on Stonington. *Connecticut Explored.* https://www.ctexplored.org/war-of-1812-stonington/

Stevenson, C. 1923. A biographical notice of the Duc de Lauzun, Commander of the Troop of Cavalry which became known as 'Lauzun's Legion' in the Revolutionary War. *The Pennsylvania Magazine of History and Biography* 47, 4, 299.

Stiles, H. R. 1891. *The History and Genealogies of Ancient Windsor, Connecticut; including East Windsor, South Windsor, Bloomfield, Windsor Locks, and Ellington 1635–1891.* Hartford, CT, Case, Lockwood & Brainard.

Surabian, D. 2012. *Preservation of Buried Human Remains in Soil.* Tolland CT, U.S. Department of Agriculture, Natural Resources Conservation Service.

Today in Connecticut History. 2019. *The Barkhamsted 'Lighthouse'.* https://todayincthistory.com/2019/12/03/december-3-the-barkhamsted-lighthouse-2/

Trocchi, J. 2007. Windsor's Palisade. *Friends of the Office of State Archaeology (FOSA) Newsletter*, Spring, 7–8.

Wadsworth, W. T. D., Bank, C.-G., Patton, K. and Doroszenko, D. 2020. Forgotten souls of the Dawn Settlement: a multicomponent geophysical survey of unmarked graves at the British American Institute Cemetery. *Historical Archaeology* 54, 624–46. https//doi.org/10.1007/s41636-020-00251-7.

Wheeler, R. A. 1900. *History of the Town of Stonington, County of New London, Connecticut, from its First Settlement in 1649 to 1900 with a genealogical register of Stonington families*. The New London CT, Day Publishing.

White, D. O. 1973. *Connecticut's Black Soldiers 1775–1783*. Chester CT: Pequot Press.

Windsor Historical Society. https://windsorhistoricalsociety.org/windsor-history/